UNDERSTANDING

DREAMS

A Dreamstairway Book

UNDERSTANDING

DREAMS

For You and Your Family

by

Ray Douglas

Dreamstairway

British Library Cataloguing in Publication Data.
A catalogue record for this book is available from the British Library.

ISBN 978-1-907091-06-3

Published in the UK by Dreamstairway

www.dreamstairway.co.uk

CONTENTS

Chapter 4   Moods and Emotions   *page 59*

Acceptance;
Affection;
Aggression;
Amusement;
Apprehension;
Arrogance;
Concern;
Contempt;
Despair;
Distrust;
Doubt;
Exasperation;
Fearfulness;
Guilt;
Hate;
Helplessness;
Horror;
Joy;
Laughter;
Love;
Painful Duty;
Pity;
Puzzlement;
Sadness;
Tearfulness;
Terror;
Worry

Chapter 5   Dream Psychology   *page 71*

The Self
The Personal Unconscious Mind
The Collective Unconscious
The Shadow
Freudian Dreams
Adlerian Dreams
Jungian Dreams
Archetypes
Collective Intelligence

INTRODUCTION

THE MORE YOU STUDY DREAMS, the more important they are apt to become. Everyday dreams about everyday affairs can grow and develop into something vastly more significant. If you are studying your family's dreams, you may find that their dreams too are becoming more important as time goes on, as though they are keeping pace with your own personal dream development. This is how they work. Our everyday thoughts and feelings have to take a back seat as the 'dreaming cycle' kicks into action and the hidden 'inner feelings', with their power of intuition, explore the contents of those parts of our minds which are normally unconscious.

This book takes the reader through the entire gamut of dream analysis and interpretation. The emphasis, perhaps, tends to be on family life, because a family unit is a rather special entity, bound together by the invisible bonds of intuition. Everybody is linked intuitionally at a very deep level, but the family especially so. Intuition is the means of knowing something about somebody else without having to be told, without having to see or hear; it is the art of communicating without words. One way to discover these golden bonds is by remembering, recording and understanding your dreams: your own personal dreams, your parents' dreams, your spouse's or partner's dreams, your children's dreams.

Dreams become more and more meaningful as we begin to understand them better. People who are spiritually orientated will find the most amazing insights through their studies, and in equal measure their lives will be directed heavenwards. Those who are not so inclined will discover the truth of Sigmund Freud's assertion, that "the interpretation of dreams is the royal road to knowledge of the unconscious activities of the mind", and discover, as Freud's associate Carl Gustav Jung discovered, that this road leads to what he called psychological individuation – the process of becoming a uniquely whole, integrated person.

CHAPTER ONE

Dreams are Important

Intuition

IN HUMANS WE CALL IT INTUITION. In animals it comes under the general heading of 'instinct'. Whatever you call it, it is a very real and powerful undercurrent that runs through the world of nature: bestowing the kind of awareness that works even when your thoughts are at rest, and your emotions are not in use. Some people are able to relax their 'hearts and minds', allow their everyday thoughts and feelings to subside, and plug in to this hidden network of awareness, becoming able to hear thoughts, to sense other people's feelings and experience their problems and worries, even to see into the future.

This may sound a bit far-fetched, and the ability to do things like this is certainly not something to be studied or practised. You would probably be wasting your time if you tried, and end up merely exercising a vivid imagination. But when you start studying your dream life, after a while the chances are you will find that this is exactly what happens in the world of dreams. Dreams are plugged in to the same wavelength as these psychic feats, because they too operate in the field of intuition, and they too occur when the everyday thoughts and emotions are at rest.

The closer you are to somebody in your waking life, especially if there is an emotional attachment, as there normally is within family circles, the more likely you are to pick up their thoughts, their feelings, their concerns, during your own dreams. If you are able to know what worries your child may be facing, for example, the better equipped you will be to do something about it. Emotional sympathy leads to empathy – the ability to experience another's feelings – which in turn leads to compassion – the ability to actually occupy those feelings and share in them. And this is the sort of unconditional warts-and-all love that makes for a closely knit, happy family.

And of course, besides the all-important family unit, by studying your own dreams you will be searching within your own deepest contents, physical, psychological and spiritual, and bringing all these things together in a harmonious way. It is only human to want to know more about yourself, what really makes you tick, and by recording, analysing and interpreting your dreams you will certainly achieve that ambition and gain the most amazing insights. Even if you can't persuade the other members of your family to do the same (and some people feel that their own dreams are a private matter and not to be shared, even with the family – or perhaps, especially with the family) your knowledge of them will be enhanced, and your bond with them will be brought that much closer.

Don't be fooled by people (especially perhaps men) who say "I never dream!". You can be sure that they do. But it often happens that people with very active brains, the intellectually orientated ones, don't like to admit that they entertain anything as illogical and uncontrolled as a dream. As soon as they wake in the morning their brains dismiss any dream memories and wipe them out, refusing to accept them. But if they too keep a dream log by their bedside, and make an effort to remember their dreams, they will surprise themselves. Explain to them that dreams do not belong to the conscious, thinking part of the brain; they belong to the intuitional, unconscious mind, and express awareness of matters so deep that even their clever brains cannot fathom them. The first dreams they record may seem to be "rubbish!", but by following the steps outlined in this book and analysing their 'rubbish', the chances are they will discover a few psychological truths about themselves.

Write Them Down

When you wake from a dream, your memory of it may well be vivid, and you can recall even the tiniest of details. But after you have got up, been to the bathroom, had your breakfast and done whatever you have to do first thing in the morning, you may well have forgotten all about it. Like King Nebuchadnezzar in the Bible, you may remember having had a dream, and that it seemed to be extremely important, but all the details have flown away. Your waking mind will have completely taken over your capacity to remember things, and dream images do not normally have first priority in people's lives. That old Babylonian king had Daniel to help him out, but the chances are that the responsibility for recording the details of your dreams lies with you alone. So the moral of that story is, write down everything you can remember about a dream as soon as you wake up – even if it is still the middle of the night. Keep a notebook (the sort that stays open where you need it to) and a pencil or ballpoint pen next to your bed and write every detail down. Don't rely on your memory alone.

Even dream incidents that seem ridiculous should be recorded in detail. The chances are they will contain truths that you need to know. Like the cryptic clues in a crossword puzzle, you may have to juggle with words and word pictures, similes and euphemisms. Dreams are full of symbols and codes which you need to crack. Take care not to exaggerate any details, or miss bits out, or improve them to make them appear more interesting or flattering. The idea is not to please your ego; the idea is to find out the deepest truths about yourself and others with whom you come in contact. Your notes must be honest. Even the bits you find embarrassing are better exposed to your own view, even if you wouldn't allow anyone else to see them, so don't let your sense of personal pride give you a false picture. Sometimes your dreams will include incidents involving other family members, and these incidents may show them in an unflattering light. Perhaps you can devise a simple code of your own rather than write their names in your book – you certainly don't want to be the cause of upsets and quarrels. But above all, your dreams are trying to show you what is happening inside your own unconscious mind, and the first aim of dream analysis is to get to know your own true self!

Analysing Dream Messages

Having written everything down in sequence, look on your dream as a story with a theme, a plot, a storyline and a conclusion – and there is bound to be more to this story than first meets the eye: you need to read between the lines. The best stories usually have more than one meaning, more than one way to understand them. There may be a story within the story; there may be any number of meanings hidden in it, and the deeper you go, the more you are likely to uncover. Dreams are made up of symbols selected by your own 'inner feelings' which reside within your unconscious mind, and your unconscious mind is an expert at using symbols. The great thing about symbols is that their meaning or significance is not fixed but depends on their context. Chapter seven of this book describes many of the most common dream symbols, and the other chapters will help you to bring out their true significance in your own context.

Once the details of a dream and their sequence are known, it is a comparatively simple matter to analyse it, whether you know the dreamer personally or not. But this is only surface analysis; to fully interpret that dream, to find out exactly what it is all about, you need to be very familiar with the dreamer's life. That is why it's often said (especially by me) that only you personally can fully interpret your own dream, because only you know about all the incidents that have taken place in your life, your recent experiences, all your history, your hopes and fears and ambitions. But in this respect your family runs a close second: you will have a very fair idea of what makes the other family members tick, and what their worries and joys happen to be.

So using your own knowledge of yourself and your family members, study the dream in sequence, taking every symbol in turn and exploring every possible meaning by thinking all round it, with the help, of course, of the other chapters in this book. If you have a reasonably 'extended' family there may be several generations of your relatives who are willing to record their dreams and allow you to analyse and interpret them. Let us take one elderly man's dream as an example of a typical 'grandfather's dream'. And at the same time may I assure you that any dream examples mentioned in this book are real and genuine. Our anonymous 'family grandfather' is an architect nearing retirement, and he has been worried by ill health – his heart has been giving him trouble, and prior to this dream he had been particularly concerned because he feared that his final project, a public building, would not be ready and completed before he died. This was his dream as he related it:

I was driving along in my car. The road was very potholed and muddy. I came to a crossroads and stopped, not sure which way to go. A railway line ran close to the road, and an empty train was standing there. The old engine was wheezing and sounded as if it were breaking down. The engine driver got out of his cab and stood there uncertainly. He was an elderly man and wore a uniform of faded red. Then another man appeared at the side of the road, a stranger, well dressed and authoritative. He introduced himself, but I immediately forgot his name. I asked him the best way to go. He got in the car with me and pointed out the best road, and I drove on. Then we came to a town and I stopped. My passenger advised me to buy some flowers, and I bought a bunch of lilies. I asked him his name again, but again I forgot it, and I murmured to myself, "This man is filling my mind with forgetfulness." As we stood there, a funeral procession came by. Then, suddenly, the people taking part in the procession stopped, abandoned whatever they were carrying, and strolled away, chatting casually among themselves. I realized that this had been merely some sort of dress rehearsal and not a real funeral.

If you refer to chapter four you will see that the emotions or moods that you have experienced during the dream, or immediately afterwards when you wake, can certainly be very significant. Grandfather said that at the beginning of the dream he was certainly very concerned and worried. Then when the mysterious stranger got in his car he felt reassurance and acceptance, and finally a strong feeling of relief as the dream came to its conclusion and he woke up.

Complicated dreams, or even apparently straight forward dreams that are not immediately obvious in their meaning, may prove much easier to understand if they are laid out on paper as a diagram or table of the sequence of events. This will allow you to insert your own comments, impressions and conclusions and the symbol meanings as given in chapter seven of this book. This is how grandfather's dream was analysed:

Driving   *A usual way of expressing life's normal journey*

Potholed road   *Currently life is not proceeding smoothly*

Crossroads   *A time of indecision or hesitation*

Empty train   *The potential means for many people to arrive at one particular place*

Old engine and driver   *His own feeling of unreliability, or inability to cater for the public's needs, because of his age*

Train driver's red uniform   *Illness, heart problems*

Authoritative stranger   *One of his archetypes, the 'Wise Man'*

Shown the best route   *His intuitive mind taking over*

Forgets stranger's name   *The Wise Man belongs to his unconscious mind, and cannot be made conscious just by wishing it*

Bought lilies   *Grandfather always associated lilies with funerals*

Watches the funeral procession   *Faces his fears and accepts the*
   inevitable

Funeral abandoned   *The event he feared, his own death, is not*
   yet imminent

Sharing Dreams

There are two ways in which dreams can be shared. The first way is fairly obvious, simply by telling other people about your own dreams and listening when they tell you about theirs. The second way is not at all obvious, and the great majority of people have never heard of such a thing, and they probably would not believe it if they did hear about it. So to take the second way first: dreams can be shared intuitionally, both people experiencing the same dream, receiving the same dream message simultaneously. And also on the intuitional level, people who have an emotional link of some sort may dream about traumatic incidents in each others' lives, past, present, or future. This happens within family circles far more often than you might think.

Affection and compassion are sentiments that often bring about intuitive dreams of this sort. I have known of numerous cases where one person's problems are experienced in a dream by someone who feels close to them emotionally. Sometimes dreams of this nature are quite literal, without the use of dream symbols, and are simply a matter of experiencing some unpleasant incident in the other person's life. The dreamer in this case actually takes the place of the other person and sees all the troublesome events through their own eyes, as though they have actually become that person and relived the event. This has certainly happened to me on more than one occasion. But usually the details of such dreams are too private and potentially harmful to be reported. Within the family circle it sometimes happens for instance that a brother or sister, or a parent, may experience a case of child bullying at first hand in this way. When this happens, careful thought and tact is needed, and it would probably be a mistake to plunge in uninvited.

Intervention may well cause worse trouble. But to be forewarned is to be forearmed, and knowledge is always a good thing to possess.

Sometimes family dreams can warn of trouble ahead, and cryptic symbols are often used by your inner feelings to express these things. There is a well known case often quoted by psychiatrists when two children dreamed that their mother had turned into a savage wolf, and a little later she was actually struck down by some violent psychiatric disorder. From my own experience, in the following example a husband dreamed of a temporary upset in his wife's behaviour which may or may not have had a good reason behind it. Only the woman herself would have been in a position to say. The dream is particularly interesting because it shows that our inner feelings, or the parts of our psyche that select dream images, are able to see into the future, and it included a pointer to show when the incident was due to take place. This was the actual dream:

I was standing on a railway station platform as a train came in, and passengers were bustling about. Then a voice said: 'Look, there's Trevor Huddleston!' I looked, and sure enough there was the tall figure of Bishop Huddleston, just off the train with his luggage. He was carrying an African child cradled in his arms. Then the dream changed, and I was in some rooms. Suddenly a rhino came charging in, knocking my things flying and trampling on everything as I dodged out of the way.

The husband went on to explain: "Bishop Trevor Huddleston was a staunch opponent of racism, and wrote the anti-apartheid book *Naught for your Comfort*. He was well known to me because I used to live in southern Africa, and I thought it was rather appropriate in my dream that he was carrying an African child. The following Sunday, a couple of days later, I was reading the paper when I came across a short paragraph: *Bishop Huddleston has arrived back in England from Africa, to take up his new appointment as...* I instantly remembered the dream and thought, 'Ha, look out for the rhino!' Almost immediately my wife rushed into the room in a furious temper. She rampaged through my things, hurling my books on the floor and down the stairs, then deliberately trampled on them. I *still* have no idea what had upset her, but she did apologize later."

One important point will soon emerge when you begin to study shared dreams, or dreams of other people's lives, or your family's experiences rather than your own: all the incidents, you will find, are *unpleasant* incidents. This is where compassion comes in again. No one needs compassion when everything is going well, when good things happen. It is not that people are being selfish, but the fact is that in the dream world nobody shares their pleasant dreams. Even those special dreams about other lives that often convince the dreamer that reincarnation is a fact (there is more about this subject in chapter six) invariably, in my experience, deal with tragedies, traumas, sadness and other unpleasant incidents that took place in that other life from long ago. So whether they reflect the past or the present, or even the future as in the last example dream, please don't wish too hard to experience shared dreams for yourself.

Children's Dreams

In ancient times people invented myths to explain their origins, and I have no doubt that many, if not all of them, originated as dreams before being written down and probably embellished afterwards. In the West we tend to know best the myths that emerged from ancient Greece, as most literary people of Europe believe that their culture arose from that source. In Britain, the myths belonging to the Celtic ancient British and the incoming Germanic tribes such as the Anglo-Saxons, tend to have been superseded in this way. In other parts of the world, of course, the indigenous people have their own myths which vary greatly from place to place. It makes quite an interesting study. But myths were rarely sheer flights of fancy. Their stories reflected the descent of mankind as they or their intuitive inner selves saw it, from primitive childlike beginnings to their own familiar way of life. If you take an interest in the idea of the great world dream (chapter six) you will appreciate the spiritual background to this descent. The story tells of the original human instincts becoming filled by all the other instincts of nature, the instincts more appropriate to animals and plants than human beings. Whether you take them to be literally true or not, these things sometimes come to the awareness of sensitive people by way of dreams and visions.

Children's dreams are of great interest because they frequently reflect the myth-making dreams of mankind throughout the ages. They often relate to the world of nature in a quite amazing way, and the world dream shows that animals and plants often represent childhood and the act of growing up. Young children obviously lack experience of the world; but if you were able to measure what I might call the 'level of spirituality' of people, you would find that children possess a much 'higher' level than most adults. To put it in religious or perhaps sentimental terms, they are 'closer to the angels' than the rest of us and are thus able to experience dreams which are not influenced too strongly by materiality, by the sophisticated influences all around us. Five year-old Andy dreamed that he ate some monkey food, and changed from a boy into a monkey. His parents of course thought immediately of 'naughty little monkey' in the sense of being mischievous, but there is a far deeper explanation to the dream than just that. In the light of the world dream, Andy had dreamed of leaving the 'young child' stage to become a 'little boy'. In other words, this was a dream of growing up in the normal way.

These are not the sort of things that most people who study dreams in the academic sense wish to hear about – they would much rather hear about evolving relationships and the development of various psychological traits. To me, however, such dreams are far more telling than the longest, most convoluted 'adult' dream of everyday relationships. Dreams of that sort will probably come soon enough, because inevitably as the conscious minds of children go through the usual learning process, as they grow older and gain more experience of the world, their dreams too will take on adult perceptions. The naive myth-making dreams of the human spiritual descent through the world of nature will normally have run their course by the time the child reaches the age of seven or eight. Increasingly after this their dreams will feature real places, and everyday exploits with their friends. And within the family circle, children too can experience intuitive dreams, when they may share something of their parents' and siblings' experiences – past, present or even future – featuring in their own dream world.You may discover too that your children are dreaming dreams that seem tailor-made for you to interpret! When that happens you may be sure that your power of intuition is fast developing; the 'collective intelligence' described in chapter five will be supervising your efforts to understand your own dream life, and overseeing your intention to interpret your family's dreams!

Drawing a Dream

It is sometimes very helpful when recording and trying to understand a dream if the dreamer makes a sketch of the dream scene as he or she remembers it, as soon as possible after waking. There are sure to be details which may otherwise be forgotten or overlooked, and a drawing will help to ensure that they are placed where their true significance lies. if you or they are an artist, of course, you may be able to produce a full-colour tableau of events; but merely a simple pencil sketch will help. It might be necessary to draw several scenes showing how the dream action progressed and changed. Try to keep the picture compact. In my experience most people when drawing their dream have a tendency to make an 'itty-bitty' drawing in which the dream symbols and actions are too small and widely scattered. On the other hand, try to resist the temptation to over-embellish the details. You should know intuitively when the picture accurately represents the dream. Remember the golden rule: be truthful to yourself (even if you prefer to pull the wool over other people's eyes!)

The example which follows is an interesting dream that was interpreted as describing one person's journey through life in the light of the great world dream (chapter six), and to assist in analysing it the dreamer, Robert, made the following sketch:

Robert dreamed he was walking in the dark carrying an electric light on a long cable plugged into the mains. He walked through a bushy field among sheep. Then the plug jerked out of its socket and the light went out, but he could still see himself walking on ahead, down a well-lit street.

In the next example John remembered a vivid dream he had experienced as a child, and which he firmly believed was an episode from a former life (see chapter six). He drew the following picture as an adult some twenty years after experiencing the dream itself:

He dreamed he was an ancient Briton on a rocky coastline. A Roman boat was in trouble a little way out and one of the young Roman soldiers came wading to the shore. John felt that he had to defend his land against these intruders, and used his spear to kill the man. The other Romans soon arrived and overpowered him.

20

Our next example recalls the myth-making dreams of long ago, when stories were woven and illustrated with the use of intuition or instinct, expressing the spiritual history of mankind. Children's dreams up to the age of seven or eight often symbolise what we could call divine truths expressed very often in humorous terms.

Simon, aged six, dreamed he went for a ride on a tall giraffe which carried him into the jungle.

Simon's drawing expresses the exuberance of childhood, and the dream itself carries an echo of the 'great world dream'. It is not entirely mere imagination: it expresses the normal process of growing up.

Dream Theatre

This is something that appeals to most children: make a play of family dreams with real people acting the parts of the dream characters. It can have the nature of a party game with friends as well as family members taking part, and it is most effective in helping to find the deepest meanings of the more complicated dreams about social relationships. It can also work well when some of the characters in the dream are not real flesh-and-blood people, but archetypes such as the wise person giving advice (he appeared in the grandfather's dream earlier in this chapter). It means that the various 'actors' can put their own interpretation on whatever they are meant to say or do, and by using their imagination can bring new insights and perhaps deeper meanings that would otherwise have escaped notice. If there are dream symbols of things, various objects, that are involved in the dream storyline, the players in this dream theatre can say whatever comes to their mind about these objects. Don't forget that the 'collective intelligence' will be supervising the game, and in the imagination of children the power of intuition is never very far away!

Questions and Answers

Some people like nothing better than to tell of their dreams and discuss them; other people however prefer to keep their dreams private, fearful of what embarrassing details may be disclosed. Families are not exempt from this. Some individuals would rather tell strangers their secrets than let their own families know about them. A group of friends can be supportive and will always give their opinions, and unless they are among that peculiar band of people who insist that all dreams are rubbish, they will offer their interpretation of dreams that have proved baffling to the dreamer. You can always get new ideas like this, and of course if you don't like those ideas you don't have to take them seriously. When people are not emotionally involved in the dream themselves, they are often in a better position to ask questions and point out connections that may otherwise elude the dreamer. But there are always likely to be images cropping up in a dream that refer to matters the dreamer would prefer to keep private, and sharing your dreams indiscriminately could cause problems.

Whether you are sharing your dreams with others or not, a dream questionnaire can be a great help. If it is your own dream, you will already have subjective feelings about it, but especially when interpreting it on your own, you need to be objective as well, looking at all the different possible shades of meaning. An impersonal dream questionnaire may help you in this respect. On your own you may well overlook some seemingly trivial component of the dream, but it may hold significance which a questionnaire will bring out. Various questionnaires are often sent out to householders these days, and this is the sort of thing you need to make, for yourself and your family members to fill in. Following are some suggestions for questions and layout:

DREAM QUESTIONNAIRE

Give a full description of the dream itself.

How important did the dream seem to be? (you might have boxes to tick, ranging from *not important at all* to *extremely important*).

If there seem to have been separate dream components, take each in turn and describe them in detail, saying how important each component seemed to be.

Describe the landscape of your dream, the surroundings, the type of ground underfoot.

23

Was there darkness in your dream, or normal daylight, or brilliant light?

Did the scene change completely during the dream? Give your ideas about this. *Very often dreams have distinct scenes, or 'dreams within dreams'.*

Did you have any strong feelings or emotions either during or immediately after the dream? *(if so, describe them as exactly as possible).*

Were other people involved in the dream? (if so, were they: *real people known to you, anonymous people who seemed unimportant, unknown people who seemed fairly important,* or *unknown people who seemed very significant*).

If the people seemed important, what were they wearing? (You will already have recorded what they did or said).

Were you taking an active part in the dream or merely looking on? *(passive, slightly active, very active).*

Were you wearing any clothes in the dream? *(dreamers often remember being naked in their dream. If this was the case, describe reactions to it, if any. If you remember wearing clothes, describe these in detail).*

Do you remember colours in the dream? *(if so, describe them, and say whether they seemed to be particularly significant).*

These are some suggestions, and I have no doubt that you will think of new questions to add to the questionnaire every time you analyse a new dream.

Another way of asking yourself or your family questions about dreams which you find baffling, is to play the game of 'free association' – the psychological method that psychiatrists may use to try to locate problem areas in a person's mind. You don't have to have psychiatric problems in order to play it! Simply make a list of all the separate elements of the dream, all the subjects and objects, setting them out in sequence. Then, (assuming that you are analysing your own dream) take each item in turn and from that starting point follow your own train of thought, your own association of ideas. First, write down everything that comes to mind, everything that the dream detail has reminded you of: happenings, characters, emotions and themes, associations past and present. Write these ideas down as though following a storyline for each item. Every new idea you come up with will probably suggest its own sequence of possible events, its own new train of thought, and continue to follow these until you run out of ideas. If you feel that any particular train of thought is becoming unpleasant, something you would rather not pursue – pursue it just the same: you could be approaching something very significant, something that your everyday mind is trying to keep hidden, and this 'something' could be the whole crux of the dream.

Even simple objects that featured in a dream may contain a cryptic clue to something more significant. Think about this dream object and say the first word, the first thing, that springs to mind. Having done that, say what *that* word reminds you of, and keep building up your train of thought until you run out of possibilities. There will always be obvious examples of word associations, such as 'black – white', 'big – little', 'sky – blue' and so on, but as the associations become more obscure, they will also become more personal, and more significant. If you find that you hesitate before giving the first word that springs to mind, if you reject that word and choose another better one, if you start feeling uncomfortable about where the associations are leading – these again are powerful hints that you may be reaching the basic foundation of the dream.

A word of warning would not out of place here: be as brutally frank as you can when interpreting your own dream; but if you are exploring someone else's dream, even your own child's dream, you will need to be very tactful and avoid hurting their feelings or damaging their sense of trust. Even within the family circle — perhaps especially within the family circle — some things are better left unsaid.

CHAPTER TWO

How Dreams Work

Who Exactly is the Dreamer?

"IN DREAMS," said the ancient sage Pippalada, "the mind beholds its own immensity". A vague comment, you might think, but it sums up the dreaming process pretty well. Our minds are certainly immensely larger than our mere thinking brains. You could say that the brain encompasses everything it can think about, which is probably the entire material universe, but the mind as a whole can encompass vastly more than just materiality: it can encompass that which is non-material as well, it can encompass the whole experience of humankind, even those matters which are completely unknown to the conscious, thinking brain and unsuspected by our sensitive emotions.

To answer the question, it is easier to say who or what is *not* the dreamer rather than who *is*. Fairly obviously, the dreamer is *not* the thinking part of the brain, no matter how clever or how stupid that brain might be; and the dreamer is fairly obviously not what we like to call the heart, or the emotional part of our brain. 'Ah well,' you might say, 'as it is not the conscious part of our brain that dreams, it must be our subconscious mind that is able to produce these dream images'. But even this cannot be right, because we will no doubt discover that our subconscious mind is what Professor Jung called the 'personal unconscious mind', and no doubt we will also soon discover that this mysterious 'one who dreams' can encompass not only the personal contents of the unconscious mind, but the impersonal or 'collective unconscious mind' as well. Your dreams can and often do produce images that were previously unknown to you, to both the conscious and the subconscious parts of your psyche.

So if you study your dream life, you will come to realise what a magical place, rather than a person, the 'dreaming self' must be. The 'self' is frequently depicted in dreams when there is an important point to be made: the self is the onlooker while events unroll before his or her eyes, and the self may take on various aspects depending on the point being made. If the self is made to observe something unsuspected, then this self – yourself – may take the form of an innocent child. Or if there is a lesson to be learnt, the self may seem to have taken the characteristics of the *attitude* your conscious self is taking to that particular situation: you may feature as a cynical person for instance, a gullible person, an aggressive person. This dream 'self' is plainly not the one who dreams. Your personality is certainly not the one who dreams. In dreams you may find that you are naked, quite as a matter of course, and nobody takes any notice of the fact. This means that 'you' in the dream are experiencing yourself without the trappings of personality, without your everyday 'disguise'.

So the dreamer is certainly not 'you'. When you, or your spouse, or your child, or your parent, says "I had a dream last night. I dreamed that I was looking at a beautiful flower floating on a lake, and then a horrible demon came out of the water..." you may realise that they are actually telling you: 'In my dream I was shown myself looking at different images of myself ...', because in fact the dreamer was being shown aspects of his or her psychic contents, different aspects of his or her own *self.* This is something that 'the dreamer' can do very easily, but it is certainly not something that the personal dreamer himself, or herself, could do. And yet a dream of this nature is doing no more than exploring what is merely subconscious, the personal unconscious mind!

I said in chapter one that the 'inner feelings' are able to select the images that make up the contents of our dreams, because these hidden feelings, which are normally unconscious, are able to be in touch intuitively with the much greater contents of the collective unconscious mind. This, I suppose, is no more than a convenient label. Even the inner feelings cannot be in direct touch with the world of spirit, which is totally impersonal, and yet we might experience dreams which seem to have come from this unfathomable area which psychology cannot approach and even religion cannot touch.

At the beginning of this chapter I quoted an ancient Hindu sage, and of course he was speaking in general terms; but it is really no use harking back to ancient times, as people exploring their dream lives sometimes do, in the hope that they will unearth the answers to these mysteries. The sad truth is that the ancients knew even less about dreams than we do now. The old Roman Cato told his son to take no notice of dreams, "since they are but the images of our hopes and fears". Perhaps he was right to advise against giving dreams the superstitious regard that was fashionable at the time, and he was certainly right in claiming that our dreams *include* our hopes and fears, but he was woefully ignorant in supposing that that is *all* they are. He was referring to the most basic, everyday, material level of dream interpretation. The brash Cato thought that he knew, and the wise Pippalada knew that he did *not* know. So I cannot say who, exactly, is the dreamer when we dream. But what I *can* say is, if you start studying and recording your dreams now, and if you encourage your family to start remembering and recording their dreams too, you will all be fellow pupils at a most unusual school; you will be the prefect, I may have written the textbook, but your dreams themselves will be the tutor.

Abstract Symbols

If you think of yourself as being made up of various constituents: your outer personality; the *ego* or personal conscious driving force; the brain with its thoughts; the 'heart' with its emotions; and your inner or hidden personality which makes up the unconscious mind: the inner feelings; the *self;* the *persona*; the *shadow*; you will see

29

that all these factors are taken into consideration when your dream images are being selected. The part of our own unconscious mind which has the final say in this selection process is that which I call the inner feelings, because it has access not only to your own memory, your past experiences, your thoughts and feelings and problems, but also to the collective unconscious mind – the great sea of past experiences and subtle solutions to mysteries common to the whole of mankind. Everything that your conscious mind has pondered over, or perhaps rejected or backed away from, is compared, matched, blended into a recognisable form, and re-presented by the inner feelings in the form of dreams, often with a psychological or purely practical solution to whatever has been troubling you.

These explanations are not cold, scientific facts which can be proved or disproved or demonstrated in a laboratory, they are merely a convenient way to classify and describe the various processes that take place. Another culture, another civilisation, might have a completely different way of describing the same things. They refer to abstract principles. Take any material object: what does it mean to you in the abstract? And what are all the incidents you can remember from the past, relating to that object? That material object is a symbol to you of all the answers you have come up with. When we try to comprehend the inner feelings, we may come to realise that this centre of understanding is able to communicate with others, with the contents of other people, on its own deep level. In some systems, the inner feelings are called the 'higher emotional centre'. They are not interested in logic or the outer forms of our personal prides and prejudices. These inner feelings 'think' or 'feel' in the abstract, and they have access not only to the contents of your own personal unconscious mind with an overview of your whole life, but also to the collective unconscious and the symbols that apply to the whole human race. Shared symbols that come to our own awareness include the Archetypes of the unconscious mind (described later in chapter five), which are able to take on a form and appearance that will be understood by you personally.

When you start recording your dreams, you may well find them to be of an everyday nature, referring to personal relationships and recent unremarkable events. Material dreams such as these may appear to lack what we have come to think of as dream symbols, but they invariably show a new aspect or a different take on the things that happen – a new way of looking at these things which turns them into symbolic rather than purely practical events. And when the process of development begins – which it certainly will when you start recording and paying attention to your dreams, they may seem to have become wholly symbolic. They will no longer refer merely to everyday events. The 'cycle of the dreaming self' will have begun in earnest, and the contents of your personal unconscious mind will begin to be shaped into recognisable forms by the inner feelings. These contents consist of everything, every impression good or bad, which has come to your attention during your waking hours. Memories of all these things sink into the unconscious mind seemingly at random. Chaotic, fragmentary, jumbled and confused, everything has to be reassembled, analysed, compared, and re-presented by the inner feelings in a way that is acceptable to the conscious mind, and inevitably this process entails the use of symbols. A dream story is an allegory, comparable to the parables told by Jesus. They paint a picture on one scale, of events and consequences relating to a different scale; they present abstract matters in material terms.

Trigger Events

People who have much to do with dreams use the term 'trigger event' to describe anything that seems to have triggered off a dream. It might be something that happened to you during the day, someone you met, something that reminded you of a previous unpleasant incident. But as you will already know, *everything* that has come to your awareness will be held in your memory banks, conscious or unconscious, and may be used by the inner feelings if it relates to something you need to know or understand. A trigger event, having made a deep impression on your conscious mind, will serve as a catalyst to your unconscious mind, bringing together any of the disjointed, disconnected or isolated memories, ideas, worries, hopes and fears that have been problematic in the past, fitting them together and making sense of them.

Anyone may suppress some unpleasant fact, or some embarrassing incident, and keep it private, locked in their memory. To take such matters a stage further, incidents sometimes become *repressed,* that is, they are wiped out of the conscious memory altogether. Matters that caused you worry or confusion during your childhood, things that seemed too horrendous to even think about, are the things most likely to have become repressed. Your conscious memory may not be able to recall them, but be assured that they are all present within the psyche, stored within the personal unconscious mind. Some trigger event may serve as a reminder of the original traumatic incident, and the inner feelings may then take the opportunity to bring these repressed memories back to your awareness. The very act of taking an interest in your own dream life may serve as the trigger, and the memory of childhood trauma may return without the need for any symbolic disguise. This may happen to a parent and a child simultaneously, but in the case of a parent it will be a time for caution; any new revelation about long-forgotten trauma needs handling very tactfully. Bringing repressed memories to awareness is an essential part of the healing process of the dreaming cycle described in the next section. Waking inspirations too, like a sudden flash of understanding, may come to you as the result of a trigger event, especially so once the continuous cycle of the dreaming self is functioning well and clearing out any unwanted material that may have become lodged within your unconscious mind.

The Dreaming Principle

The easiest way to understand the principles involved when a person dreams, is to visualise yourself in the abstract, non-material sense. Forget about your body for a minute, and think of a bubble, or a sphere, or a planet floating in space, then imagine that this floating ball is your own disembodied self, your astral self perhaps, gently drifting along. Imagine that your translucent upper surface and all its contents are bathed in the light of the sun, while your lower surface, your underside, and all its contents are cloaked in darkness. The upper side will represent yourself during the day when you are wide awake and experiencing all the happenings that keep your mind occupied. The lower side equals night time, when you are sound asleep and your thoughts and emotions have shut down for the night.

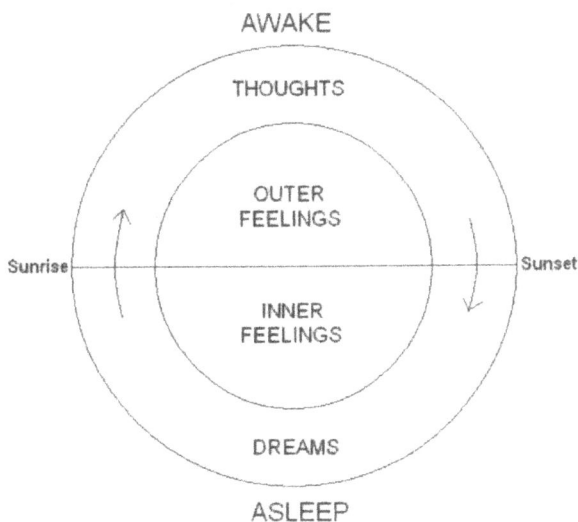

The cycle of sleep, when the outer feelings become inner feelings, and thoughts change into dreams. The function of emotions is to evaluate. Your thoughts may know the cost of everything, but it needs your emotions to decide the true value. In sleep the inner feelings assess jumbled thoughts and impressions, and reassemble them into a useful form using symbols which are then re-presented to your waking awareness by way of dreams.

When you look at the diagram on the previous page, think of it as a diagram of yourself in the abstract. Life is a constant cycle, although, like the shadow cast by a sundial gnomon, it may not seem to be constantly on the move. Remember that you are being compared to a planet floating around the sun in space. Everything is in motion, so think of yourself in this diagrammatic form as a clock registering the hours of day and night, waking and sleeping. A horizon separates day from night, waking from sleeping. You don't really go to sleep at six in the evening and wake up at six in the morning, as the diagram would suggest. You may even work a night shift or otherwise differ from the norm, but in this sense, 'day' is when you are awake, and 'night' is when you are asleep. Dawn is on the left of the horizon, noon or the time when you are widest awake is at the top, dusk is on the right, and midnight or the time when you are most soundly asleep, is directly underneath.

Now, to take it a stage further, think of your wide awake self as your conscious mind, and your sleeping self as your unconscious mind. When you fall asleep, all the thoughts and emotions and experiences that have occupied your conscious mind during the day, sink down into your unconscious mind where they are mingled with all the *other* contents of that largely unknown region of the psyche. All this material you could say becomes food for your personal unconscious mind, to be digested and assimilated. We are so used to the workings of our conscious, thinking minds that we tend to take them for granted. What we sometimes fail to realise is that all these thoughts and feelings, even things you might think had been completely forgotten, even things which you turned away from, things which you pretended not to notice, things that you would rather not know about, they all sink, jumbled, into the great receptacle of the unconscious mind. Your warm emotions are said to be the seat of value judgement: your ordinary emotions or feelings decide the worth, the abstract, aesthetic value of things, like their beauty and their ability to give pleasure: their value rather than their cost. Your cold thinking brain or thoughts are responsible for finding out the cost of things rather than their abstract value.

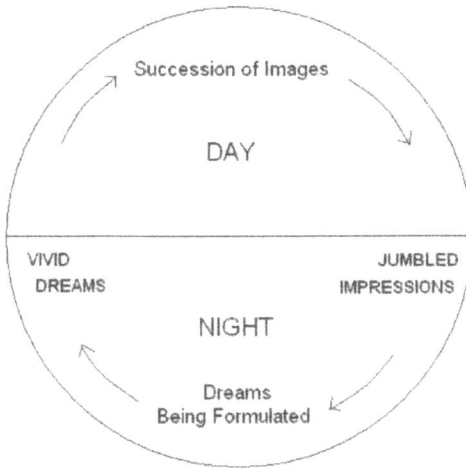

If you wake soon after falling asleep, remembered dreams are liable to be jumbled or fragmented, never quite making sense. As the sleeping period wears on, dreams become formulated more clearly. The most vivid dreams arrive at or just before dawn.

The Inner Feelings

When you are asleep, your thinking brain may have shut down, but this is when, as the sage Pippalada put it, 'the mind beholds its own immensity'. Your waking feelings give way to the *inner feelings*, and your waking thoughts give way to *dreams*. At the end of the day, you could say, when your mind is tired, all the thoughts and impressions of the day are jumbled together, and in this jumbled state they are presented to the darkness of the unconscious mind. Consequently, when you doze fitfully in the evening before going to bed (I know I do!) you will have a lot of little dreams, and perhaps they will seem to be making sense *at the time*, but when you snap back into wakefulness again, you will find that those snatches and dribs and drabs of dreams are in fact quite

35

chaotic. They will be jumbled, and if you think about them they will probably seem like complete nonsense to your conscious mind. And this is exactly what they are: they have not yet had time to be assembled into a form which makes any sort of sense.

Your inner feelings are the inner seat of value judgement, and these hidden feelings sort out all your jumbled, chaotic thoughts and emotions, and examine them for their true worth. They compare them with all that has gone before, analyse them, see how they fit in to your life, and set them out in the way that will be of most value to you personally, and to the way they interact with your family and friends. In some cultures the inner feelings are called the 'higher emotional centre', and with very good cause. They are able to see the value of things that have been missed by your ordinary 'emotional centre'. They are something like the British House of Lords with their greater experience of life, pointing out the mistakes and shortcomings of the ordinary House of Commons, though they cannot actually legislate on their own. They use symbols to explain matters that cannot otherwise be put into words and images, and because they operate in the field of intuition, they have access to the inner feelings of other people too: they also have access to the immense psychic ocean of wisdom that is called the collective unconscious mind. And as these subconscious emotions are being sorted and formulated, during your period of sleep, into unexpressed thoughts, they come to your conscious awareness in the form of dreams.

Workings of the Unconscious Mind

The Chinese in their ancient philosophical system formulated the principle of yin and yang, and this represents a useful way of thinking about the unconscious mind. They considered it in terms of male and female: the male, or conscious mind, is compared to a channel, and what is channelled in this case are all the impressions, thoughts and feelings of the day. The female, or unconscious mind, is compared to a vessel receiving that which has been channelled, and creating something new out of this material, nurturing it, and giving birth to a completely new creation. The male – yang – is the bright, upper, waking side of the self. The female – yin – is the dark, mysterious, creative side of the self. The light part curves and extends some way into the dark zone, representing the evening, and the dark part curves and extends an equal way into the light zone, representing dawn. Consciousness contains a small part of the unconscious within itself, represented as a black spot within the white, and in equal measure the unconscious mind contains a small part of consciousness within itself, as a white spot within the black. And of course, this is a very accurate picture of the process constantly taking place within us all.

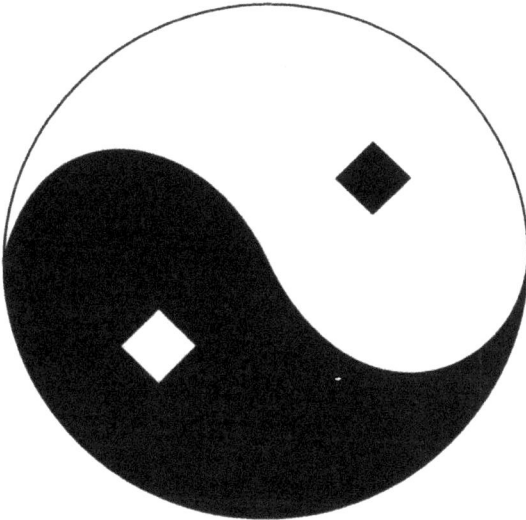

Yin and yang. The bright consciousness of the yang and the dark but receptive body of the yin.

I mentioned earlier that unpleasant memories can become repressed, or banished from the conscious memory, especially during childhood, and which may be brought back to awareness by some trigger event. But *any* unpleasant experience or horrific piece of information, or some feature or characteristic about yourself that would rather not have, and would prefer to keep hidden from the public gaze – any or all of these things will have sunk down into the personal unconscious mind which people commonly call 'the subconscious'. The inner feelings do a marvellous job of integrating all the factors which can be integrated, putting everything into an acceptable form which will not clutter up your mind with unwanted material. But even this 'higher emotional centre' can find some things which cannot be resolved for the time being, which cannot be assimilated and projected back into your normal thinking and feeling. And these dark contents inevitably remain within the depths of the personal unconscious mind. This is especially true of people who have not studied their dream life, and in particular those who do not care to relax their thoughts and principles: those people who tend to be 'uptight', and who keep their faults and weaknesses very private. There is nothing wrong with that, of course, within reason. The danger starts when people keep these things private even from themselves, and refuse to face their own psychological contents.

But these things do not disappear because we disown them: they remain within our own personal unconscious mind, in the dark depths of the yin, and there they sink as though with the force of gravity, untouched even by the inner feelings, washed over by the stream of inner thoughts – our dreams – and like some unpleasant disease in the body they grow in size and strength, gathering fresh material from time to time. These things may be difficult to be absorbed into meaningful dreams, they may not fit in harmoniously with our everyday concerns, but sooner or later they will be stirred by the inner feelings, picked up by the stream of dreams, and emerge in the form of a nightmarish figure, like the fictitious evil Mr Hyde who emerged from the good Dr Jekyll. Fortunately, if we study our dream lives sincerely and accept our own psychic contents as truly our own, rather than an undeserved attack from some outside force, these things will resolve themselves peacefully enough. This creature of nightmares was dubbed 'the shadow' by professor Jung, and this name is a very apt description.

CONSCIOUS MIND

YOUR IDEAL SELF

YOUR SHADOW SELF

UNCONSCIOUS MIND

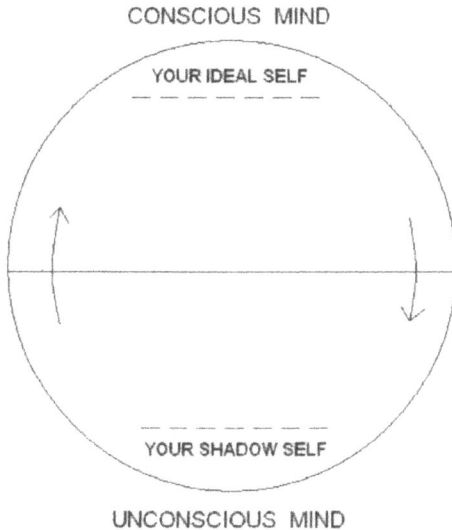

Your ideal self is the unattainably perfect you. Your shadow self consists of everything you don't want to accept about yourself.

Children are innocent and inexperienced in the bad ways of the world, and yet they too may well accommodate 'the shadow' within their own personal unconscious minds. You would not really expect young children to have all sorts of dark secrets hidden away in this fashion, but childhood is the time of life when unpleasant thoughts and feelings become repressed, and the 'bones' of dream demons are being created, to be fleshed out more and more as time progresses. Later in the book (chapter five) the section on 'Adlerian Dreams' may help to explain why and how unpleasant experiences can become locked into a child's unconscious mind, only to be released much later, perhaps in the form of dreams, perhaps taking the form of worrying behaviour which does not seem to have any good cause. The 'shadow' can also explain why children sometimes suffer from the 'night terrors' – screaming nightmares which are not remembered by the child in the morning. During sleep the 'shadow' may make its frightening presence known, but still refuses to emerge into the daylight. If this sort of thing happens, don't worry. Please don't jump to conclusions as to the causes, either. If something is wrong, loving acceptance is a more effective medicine than worry and nagging. Encourage your child to remember his or her dreams, and make a careful note of them all.

Evening Dreams and Dawn Dreams

Having seen how all the thoughts and impressions of the day sink jumbled down into the darkness of the personal unconscious mind, we can see clearly why those dreams we experience early on during the period of sleep, tend to be somewhat chaotic and jumbled themselves. Like the 'dozing' dreams that you may well experience when you fall asleep for a few moments, in the evening perhaps, or after a meal, they will prove impossible to analyse successfully, let alone lend themselves to sensible interpretation. They will not have not had time enough to be sorted into any useful form by the inner feelings. The most meaningful and perfectly formed dreams will emerge towards the end of the sleeping period, and really special 'great dreams' will appear at dawn. You will appreciate that the inner feelings could be said to be the seat of wisdom: dawn dreams are timed to occur just before you wake up in the morning. At this time they are most likely to be remembered, and have the greatest impact on your conscious awareness. Be very sure that dawn dreams are really important. They will carry a message that needs to be heard and understood by your everyday mind, your thoughts and feelings.

This is not to say that *all* dreams occurring at this time are of the greatest importance, but even when they are not, they will be the best that can be done with the material available. They will have been assembled and formulated and symbolised from all the thoughts and feelings which need to be sorted and symbolised, and perhaps ninety percent of their material will relate to your experiences of the previous day. Dreams in between evening and morning, on a sliding scale, will have been assembled from the same material, and will be increasingly significant as the period of sleep progresses. If there are lessons to be learnt, or possible solutions of problems to be pointed out, they too will gather significance as the night passes. This means that if you wake from a dream in the middle of the sleeping period, your dream is less likely to have reached a satisfactory conclusion; it is more likely to be worrying and cause you anxiety, because problems will have been identified by the inner feelings, projected in dream form, but a solution to whatever the worry may be has not yet been formulated. That is the ideal scenario, though there will be so many unknown factors involved in any particular case that it is impossible to be dogmatic about it: there will always be exceptions.

Light and Deep Sleeping periods

You will probably be familiar with 'rapid eye movement', also known as REM. This is when the sleeper's eyelids can be seen to be moving and flickering as his or her eyes, though closed in sleep, seem to be darting about as though peering around in a state of excitement. These are the periods of lightest sleep, and it has often been said that dreams only occur during these REM episodes. But I am saying that this is a misconception: I believe that the deepest dreams tend to occur during the periods of deepest sleep, when there is no eyelid movement. The most likely explanation is that REM periods concern the 'lightest' dreams in the psychological and the spiritual sense. The dreamer is 'looking outwards' rather than 'looking inwards', and REM dreams will prove to relate to everyday matters and relationships. They will contain the fewest cryptic symbols and more closely resemble the dreamer's everyday waking thoughts. The most significant dreams, it will be discovered, are those which occur during the periods of deep sleep. The deep sleep cycle is the one that normally precedes waking, and the most vivid dawn dreams will have been experienced during this period. Non-REM dreams are unlikely to bear any relationship to everyday, mundane events except to the extent that those events have served to trigger the dream itself.

It is during rapid eye movement sleep that outside influences can readily intrude on the dreaming awareness, when voices or other sounds or sensations from the outside world can become incorporated into a dream. If you want to put ideas into someone's mind, this is one way to do it. If your pre-teenage child likes to play with matches for instance, you can lean close to the child during their rapid eye movement sleeping phase, and say, slowly and firmly: "Remember fire!". During the REM phase the child will probably be dreaming of everyday incidents, and your voice will enter into the dream as a voice 'from above', and will certainly be remembered. But you have to be very careful and responsible here. Make what you say a reminder. Never issue general commands, never say something like "Do as your told!" If you do this it will probably have a very unfortunate psychological effect, and cause problems with your child's relationships later. By implanting a command into the child's subconscious mind you would be behaving like a stage hypnotist, without the ability to rescind the command. You may well undermine the child's growing confidence and steer him or her in the wrong direction. Imagine the possibly tragic consequences of your child growing up believing they have to obey whatever anyone told them to do, right or wrong! You have the ability to influence your child's behaviour in a positive and constructive way. Please do not abuse that privilege.

CHAPTER THREE

Pigeonhole Your Dreams

Personal and Everyday Dreams

WHEN SETTING OUT first to analyse and then to interpret any dream, it is a good idea to decide what type of dream it is, what category it belongs to. It may, and probably will, relate to everyday events and the people you meet and places you visit daily. A dream of this sort can really only be interpreted fully by the dreamer personally, because only he or she can know all the ins and outs of their everyday lives and their own ideas, thoughts and feelings. It may very likely be a dream that deals with your relationships with other people, and how they interact with you. Then again, if you are a person with firm attitudes and morals, it may have been the sort of dream that compensates and balances out your habitual attitudes, by portraying you acting out the opposite extreme. It may be a dream that expresses some worry that has been nagging you. It may even be a dream that keeps recurring, returning to the same theme again and again, night after night. It may have been a terrifying nightmare which leaves you in a cold sweat. Another possibility is that you may have become conscious and aware during the dream although in fact you were still sound asleep. Or it might have been an intuitional dream mysteriously allowing you to experience something of other people's lives.

Probably ninety percent of dreams in general could be called personal and everyday dreams, because that is what they seem to portray. They seldom seem to have a constructive message to offer, they simply reflect your daily affairs, and in this respect perhaps old Cato was right when he maintained that dreams were 'simply the images of our hopes and fears'. But may I say now, never leave a dream at that, never assume that the dream has no meaning beyond the obvious. Even though the various things that featured in an everyday dream are everyday objects and occurrences, they are still 'symbols' as far as the inner feelings are concerned. Treat them as dream symbols: look up any hidden or psychological meanings that may be attached to these things, and think all round them. This is the way to encourage your own inner feelings, and those of your family members, to respond in a far deeper, more meaningful way. When the flavour of your dreams seem to have changed, it means that the 'dreaming cycle' has begun in earnest, cleaning out any unpleasant thoughts and emotions that may have been clogging up your personal unconscious mind, clearing the air by putting all these things into a new and clearer light in the form of meaningful dreams. Because dreams may seem fairly meaningless, never despair and assume that you must be a meaningless person! You have amazing depths, and your insight and power of intuition are waiting to be woken by the inner feelings and brought into awareness.

Relationship Dreams

Your relationship with all the other people with whom you come into contact is probably a very important matter to you. It certainly is to most people, though some others may be reclusive, preferring their own company to the social round. I would not like to say that one is right and the other wrong, it takes all sorts to make a world. People who tend not to mix are often the observers of the world, watching how others tick. Because they communicate less, talk less, good mixers may well assume that quiet, private people are lacking in thoughts and ideas. In fact, the opposite is usually the case. Because they never waste their energy in conversation and debate, they may be highly skilled in cause and effect, insight and intuition. Some people prefer their own company through choice. Others may long to socialise more than they do, but feel inhibited or shy. This brings us to a very important point: inhibitions belong to the outward emotions. The inward emotions, the inner feelings, have no inhibitions at all. In our dreams we have no inhibitions. Where we might understandably hesitate to tread in our waking life, our dreaming selves will happily venture into what to the waking self might appear a threatening or daunting situation. We can see this by the fact that many people dream that they go about their daily affairs and interactions with friends and strangers, whilst naked; one might expect habitual nudists to dream that they are unclothed in public, but this is true even in the case of people who would probably rather die than appear naked in public!

Following from this, if you are normally somewhat inhibited in your relationship with any person – your employer, perhaps – in your dream when your inhibitions have fallen away, you may see yourself interacting with that person in the way you would like to in real life, if only you dared! This point is worth remembering when interpreting a relationship dream. When Sigmund Freud set out his ideas regarding dreams, sex was a somewhat taboo subject in society, and this fact quite understandably coloured his analyses and interpretations of dreams, and explained the great importance he set upon attitudes towards sex. When there is a great taboo in people's lives, as a consequence they may well feel guilty if they have desires and urges that seem to go against that social taboo, and these feelings are bound to give rise to dreams. Sex at that time was a great cause of imbalance within the personal unconscious mind. Nowadays, moral and social rules are much more relaxed in this respect. But there are still moral imbalances and social dissatisfactions today, when sex comes to the forefront of dreams.

The fact is, it is rare nowadays for anyone to dream of their sex lives or their personal attitude towards sex, unless there really is some kind of sexual imbalance and dissatisfaction with personal relationships. If you are quite happy in all respects with your own sexual contents and the way in which you habitually cope with your own sexual instincts, you ought not to be dreaming about them. They will not appear as a problem to be solved by the inner feelings. Sexual dreams, then, point to some need for a change of habits, and possibly a more open outlook as regards morality. Morality is very important to the inner feelings, but only as far as it adversely affects your own psychological integrity. Dreams of sex may be pointing out the need for greater broad-mindedness: beware of hurting other's feelings by criticising their sexual habits during your waking life. Remember the intuitional interaction that goes on behind the scenes. By upsetting them, you may be disrupting your own psychic balance, a fact which will certainly be reflected in your dreams.

Relationship dreams will become fewer as your own dream-life develops, and analysing and interpreting dreams becomes routine for you. Your dreams will then concentrate on your own psychic contents. In a sense, you will become more selfish! Not as far as material possessions are concerned, but once your relationship with others is no longer a cause of inner concern, the dreaming cycle can proceed with its own true purpose – making the dreamer a better, more complete, more integrated person, by clearing out unwanted material, by bearding the demonic 'shadow' in his dark lair and making him a respectable, acceptable part of your own understanding. No part of yourself will then be hidden from your own view, and as the oracle said: "Know thyself!"

Balancing Out Lives

The dreaming process works naturally in the long-term to bring about a balanced personality, levelling out extremes. This is the type of thing that stands out most clearly in a family environment. In a completely balanced personality, for instance, one's feelings for others will be balanced by one's feelings for oneself, though these may not *necessarily* be warm or friendly feelings; indeed, they may range between the extremes of love and hate. The main point about 'balance' is that the attitudes we apply to ourselves *should* be applied to others in equal measure, and dreams often point out the somewhat inevitable discrepancies in this respect.

Balance works in other ways too: some people may go through life peacefully and unadventurously, never acting in an unkind or aggressive manner – but their dreams may sometimes seem full of daring exploits and involve an alarming degree of violence and passion. The opposite type of people who seem to live constantly on the edge of their nerves, hyperactive perhaps, quick to pick a quarrel or fly into a rage, may experience dreams of gentle pursuits, peace and harmony.

In my own experience, siblings often feel competitive and in trying to gain an advantage sometimes give the impression that they dislike one another – especially brothers, perhaps. This type of behaviour is really at the top-edge of the personality rather than something deep-rooted that needs clearing out by means of the dreaming process. Brothers may say spiteful things to one another, but they don't really mean it! They are more likely to be well balanced in their relationship than unrelated friends are. And so a well-balanced person is not necessarily a friendly, or even a *good* person in the generally-accepted sense of the word, though morals will be found to feature prominently in balancing dreams. Over-virtuous people frequently dream of behaving in a thoroughly immoral manner, while at the other extreme an undisciplined person who cares little for the rights of others may dream of discipline, morality and justice. Striking a balance within the cycle of the mind – giving and taking, conscious and unconscious – is a basic function of the inner feelings finding expression by way of the dreaming self. Religious feelings too, whether positive or negative, or a lack of appreciation of spiritual matters, these sentiments are often balanced out in dreams that may appear baffling – dreams which, it seems, can only be intended to stretch the dreamer's waking mind and provoke creative thought.

Life-balancing dreams are in some ways related to wish-fulfilment dreams in that they tend to express the dreamer's hopes and longings, and when you read chapter five you may see that they resemble Adlerian dreams in that they express the dreamer's wish to experience qualities they do not normally possess. The old childhood problem of bullying may feature strongly in this type of dream, when the tables become turned and the bully becomes the bullied. A normally gentle person may dream of inflicting violence; in the same way a chaste person may dream of sexual indulgence. A dream of this nature is unlikely to contain much in the way of useful information, but it may provide simple psychological release and a broader outlook. The pioneer psycho-analysts Freud, Adler and Jung, each in their own way, thought of dreams as possessing a great healing potential, and certainly they can lead to the removal of much psychological clutter, resulting in a healthier psyche. But any dream that points out negative reactions and features unpleasant emotions will function as a healing dream, if the hint is taken by the dreamer. We all benefit from a positive attitude towards life with its ups and downs.

Worrying Dreams

You may of course have some nagging worry in your waking mind, and your dream may well reflect this fact; you may well dream that the cause of the worry has taken on a solid form which features as an adversary of some kind. A purely abstract problem in real life can take on a menacing form, human, animal, or unnamed threat lurking around the corner. On the other hand, particularly if your worries mean that you are not sleeping well, the dreams themselves may well be fragmented and nonsensical, similar to the dreams you usually experience when briefly dozing off. But when there is no obvious cause for worried feelings, when the sense of extreme worry permeates your dream, it is as well to pay careful attention to the dream itself and analyse it very thoughtfully. It may reflect some imbalance in the personal unconscious mind, when the negative outweighs the positive. It may involve the personal shadow – made up of all the worrying or unpleasant experiences and thoughts in your past – having grown to a certain size and taking on what seems like a life of its own. It is time to record and interpret your dreams in earnest! Your demonic shadow cannot harm you, by the way, because it is already a part of your own psyche – a part you would be far better off without.

Worry as a dream feature may come about when circumstances have forced you to 'live a lie', for whatever reason. When you feel obliged to act a part which is not really the true you; when you find yourself unable to follow your own true nature, your own real character, whether this happens to be 'good' or 'bad' in everybody else's eyes. There are times probably in everybody's life when your brain seems to be in a whirl, even when you have no idea why. When this happens, the feeling is sure to transfer itself to your dream life, if only temporarily. But in the normal way, as we are now well aware, evening or dozing dreams tend to be rather chaotic and meaningless at the best of times, but the dreaming process settles down and the dreams that are produced later in the night, and particularly just before dawn are far more sensible and positive.

A sense of disorientation that persists in your dreams, even in dreams which happen at the end of the sleeping period, may accompany the feeling that you have indeed lost your way in some major sense, whether physically, socially, morally, or career-wise. Any traumatic situation such as this is sure to feature in your dreams. You are fortunate because your inner feelings may be better equipped to deal with your sense of aimlessness than your waking mind. You will have become aware of this deep faculty that we all possess, and your dream may be showing you what can be done about the problem. Remember and think round every detail of the dream, particularly if it was vivid and you experienced it towards dawn.

What we might call a disaster dream when everything seems to be going wrong, is something very like a nightmare; whatever the general subject matter, disaster itself, you could say, sometimes seems to be the emotional theme forming a background to your dream. If there are recognizable events, look at each of these separately and try to identify the problem in each case; if there is a common theme, a common cause, this will be the important factor. If the dream events do not make sense at all, and seem mere excuses for the sense of disaster to continue, take it as a hint that you are living under stress. You need to adopt a more relaxed view of life, and perhaps take a more submissive attitude – submissive, that is, to fate; an acceptance that 'what will be, will be'. It is of little use to worry over things you cannot control. So-called anxiety neurosis is at the root of most worrying dreams that seem to be inexplicable, and your newly discovered inner feelings are there to help you overcome these problems.

It is rather worrying when your dream seems disgusting in some way. It is in the nature of the inner feelings to express all the unwanted or unpleasant experiences, thoughts and feelings and habits, all those unresolved problems that pass down into the personal unconscious mind, in symbolic form, as actual dirt that needs throwing away. As always, you will need to think around all the dream features very carefully. They should give you a clue as to the source of whatever you found disgusting. You will be able to find out whether the unpleasant situation is a 'one-off' or a regular ongoing circumstance; an aspect of yourself, or perhaps a family member. A toilet situation that has become disgusting in some way is a common dream theme, and usually refers to some feature in your own personality which you do not like and would be better off without. Now you are familiar with the cycle of dreams, you are in a position to realize if and when, and in what way, the disgusting dream element is related to your own subtle contents. Your dream life is working towards your own betterment, and so is less likely to be concerned with someone else's psychic problems or moral shortcomings, even other family members, although family responsibilities may certainly play a part.

Recurring Dreams

Sometimes the same dream, or one very similar, comes to the dreamer night after night, recurring again and again, like an old-fashioned gramophone with the needle stuck in one track. The dream is trying to tell you something, but do you really need telling over and over? A genuinely recurrent dream is referring to something akin to a psychological block that is keeping you off balance and hindering the smooth progress of the dreaming cycle. But there is one very important thing to bear in mind: you may *dream* that a dream is recurring when in fact it is not; it often happens that you dream that some sequence of events has occurred by way of the dreaming process many times before, but this is all part of the dream narrative, part of the story. Then again some people bend the truth a little and *say* that a dream has been recurring when in fact they know it has not. Perhaps they feel that recurrence adds weight or importance to their dream, especially when they interpret it as warning them of some future event. Most people like the idea of dreaming about the future, but in fact, dreams warning us of future events are unlikely to recur: nine times out of ten they will be once for all warnings. You may take it from this that truly recurrent dreams are not at all common. Typically, a truly recurrent dream stems from within the dreamer's own mind, highlighting a psychological quirk that needs pointing out. A dream of this nature is usually fairly uncomplicated. If you can interpret it, please take it to heart, because it is indeed a 'warning dream', but of an *inside* event, and one that needs urgent attention.

Nightmares

The original meaning of a nightmare, also known as a night-hag, or 'the riding of the witch', was not simply a bad dream. The old English 'mare' was a kind of evil spirit which terrorised sleeping people, and the word 'nightmare' described a physical sensation as though a weight had been placed on the chest, resulting in the feeling of being crushed. This could be symptomatic of a medical problem, and may be caused by the condition called 'apnoea' when breathing ceases to be automatic and stops long enough to cause a lack of oxygenated blood to the heart – in effect a minor heart attack. It may or may not be accompanied by an actual bad dream. The inner feelings may make use of the event to present a real problem in frightening symbolic terms. More usually the term 'nightmare' is used simply to describe a terrifying dream, which may well have been triggered by some real-life event. Children especially are sometimes apt to experience the 'night terrors' when they may call out or scream and thrash about while still asleep, though in the morning that may have no recollection of any actual dream. The majority of bad dreams however arise from the normal cycling process of the dreaming self. Any problem currently being experienced may well be symbolised in a dream as being chased by some unknown danger. If it does involve a frightening apparition unrelated to any actual problems, it will probably stem from the personal shadow – the compartment deep within the personal unconscious mind where all the unresolved problems have been accumulating during your life, and this shadow seems to have taken on a life of its own. Recording, analysing and interpreting your dreams will solve the problem eventually.

Sleep paralysis can be a frightening phenomenon – a state that could be said to be half way between sleeping and waking, when you want to wake fully but cannot move a muscle. You experience the totally helpless feeling of being paralysed. This highly unpleasant sensation is sometimes linked to lucid dreaming in which you become aware that you are dreaming. This sort of dream is described in the next paragraph. During most lucid dreams the dreamer is able to manipulate the dream characters and events, but sleep paralysis prevents this happening. If it could be called a dream, sleep paralysis seems to be expressing the wish to alter physical characteristics which cannot be altered in practice. When it occurs in the course of a dream, it certainly implies helplessness to act without first allowing the dream events to be completed. This can sometimes be linked to an unpleasant real-life situation which must be allowed to run its course before finding a solution – a solution at which the dream itself may hint.

Lucid Dreams

It sometimes happens that you become aware that you are asleep and dreaming, and this is known as a 'lucid dream'. You will then discover that you are able to control the events in your dream, making the dream characters do what you want them to do, and even allow yourself to travel around at will. Some dream books recommend encouraging this faculty in yourself and even making a habit of it. The result may well be to boost your self confidence and strengthen your own ego. But if you are take your dream life at all seriously and hope to learn from it, to become a better more integrated person, to understand your family's needs and hopes and fears, I have to advise against the practice. If a lucid dream happens, all well and good. But please don't think that it is a good idea to encourage dreams of this kind. Dreams are meant to be orchestrated by the inner feelings, and not the ego. The personal ego has all day to put its ideas forward and should be allowed to sleep at night; allow the inner feelings to do their proper job!

I am claiming that the ultimate aim of our dreams and the dreaming process is to clear out the dark contents of the personal unconscious mind before these contents become too heavy a spiritual and psychological burden. This is a function of the Inner feelings, which are not controlled by our thinking, reasoning minds. Our everyday ego cannot assist in the process, much as it would like to. When you experience a lucid dream, use it to your own advantage: to be forewarned is to be forearmed; you will still be asleep, but conscious of what is happening. Allow the dream events to unfold without interference, go along with it like a character in a play, and you may be amazed at what you will learn.

The only exception to this rule is when somebody – particularly a child – is having bad dreams every night and you cannot understand why this should be, you might then encourage him or her to make the dream lucid. Tell them to remember that the frightening experience is 'only a dream', and if they can remember that they are asleep when they are actually having the next bad dream, they can take over the action if they want to. If they are being chased by some frightening figure in the dream, tell them that they should be able to make that figure turn round and run the other way. Or they might be able to confront the frightener boldly, let it come up to them and find out what it wants, and in this way they will be able to lose their fear of the dream.

Making Dreams Happen

I have often said how important it is to let the dream run its course, allowing it to have its say without interference from the conscious ego. But it may be that you have experienced a frustratingly inconclusive dream and feel sure that a further dream, a sequel or extension of the first, would give you a satisfying answer. The way to encourage this is to quieten your thoughts and emotions when you are ready for sleep. There is no need to concentrate on the subject, or think hard about it. Simply feel that there is an empty space in your own psyche, a space which is waiting to be filled by a dream. Your inner feelings are not something *less* than your brain, that they need to be told about it. They will already know of the need, ahead of your conscious mind. In quietness you are *asking* yourself for the required dream; if you try to *tell* yourself, the result may be a lucid dream or a wish-fulfilment dream which is liable to give you false or misleading answers.

Another way of 'extending' a dream in the hope that it will provide a more satisfactory conclusion, is to practice what is known as 'dream re-entry'. You might try this when you feel that a dream has been cut short for some reason, if you feel that an important answer was about to emerge when you woke up, if you want to know *what happened next*. The technique is to relax and make yourself comfortable, with eyes closed, and feel as though you are drifting off to sleep while still remaining awake. The original dream will still be on your mind, and you visualise it, relive it, let it run its course in your mind, and when it reaches the 'end' allow it to continue as long as it will. The idea is not to make your dream lucid in the sense of manipulating it, but to quieten your own thoughts and feelings and allow it to run its full course without interference. But bear in mind that it is no use trying to control the dream yourself, or any conclusion will have arisen from your own desires.

People who practice dream therapy professionally use the term 'incubating dreams' to describe concentrating on the subject before you go to sleep, so as to encourage the dream you want to happen. Personally, I am not at all sure that this is a good idea: it should be remembered that dreams of any value arise from images selected by the hidden inner feelings, and not from the ego, or from the everyday emotions, or the thinking part of the brain. A powerful ego can quite easily take the stage and overrule the deeper – or higher – aspects of your own psyche; if you *wish* for a dream, this is what will happen. If you try to *command* a dream, your everyday thinking mind will produce one for you. This is no problem for the ego, for your thinking mind, but the result will be what is known as a wish-fulfilment dream which will be of no use whatsoever. Think about any problems you may have, by all means, and *submit* them or offer them to your innermost self with a feeling of trust. If your child has a problem and would like a dream to help solve it, you can encourage them to write the problem down and 'post' it under their pillow, but tell them not to bother too much about it. If you are too determined about it, too passionate, you will simply encourage your conscious mind. your ego, to intervene in any resultant dream.

A dream involving the dreamers' own willpower, a deliberately induced dream intended to supply information – this represents a dream-trip to nowhere. The hidden inner feelings need to be able to select the images and symbols which go to make up your dreams, clearing out the clutter within your own personal unconscious mind. The higher emotional centre known as the inner feelings cannot be coerced. And what is a 'wish-fulfilment dream'? When somebody wishes fervently for some outcome, or has fears about their fate, they are liable to dream that their wishes have come true – quite falsely, as it transpires. A starving person may dream of food that never actually appears. This is because their conscious desires, their ego, has forced an entry into the closed territory of the personal unconscious mind and taken over the dreaming process, hoping to influence events. The normal dreaming process by way of the inner feelings will have been usurped, or short-circuited, and there is nothing to be gained by such a dream except false hope.

Intuitional Dreams

Dreams of this sort empathise with another person. When the inner feelings are approaching awareness, that is, less *unconscious*, intuition becomes quite open, allowing the thoughts and feelings of one to be experienced by others. This characteristic is equally pronounced by way of dreams, and dreaming about the waking-life experiences of others, particularly perhaps of family and friends, becomes a common experience. There is a strong connection between intuitional dreams of living people whom you know, and reincarnation dreams about dead people whom you did not know. Dreams during which you dream of previously unknown facts, incidents, places and people, all of which later turn out to be completely true, are known as 'veridical' dreams. Always of great interest, such dreams usually follow some traumatic incident involving not the dreamer personally but the object of the dream, or a close emotional involvement between the dreamer and the person being dreamed about. They are frequently dawn dreams, and depend upon the principles of empathy, sympathy, and compassion on the part of the dreamer, which in their turn depend on a well-balanced psyche.

Any dream in which the dreamer finds that he or she has become someone else is a 'non'-self' dream. It will seem to have been dreamed on behalf of someone else, experiencing someone else's problems and traumatic incidents. Occasionally such dreams may experience an incident in the life of an animal. I have known vivid dreams of this sort that have convinced the dreamer of the reality of reincarnation. But it should be remembered that the inner feelings which are normally responsible for assembling dream images, also have open contact with the inner feelings of other creatures, and on a non-material plane neither space nor time are necessarily barriers to shared images. Great stuff! This is the sort of dream liable to infuriate excessively intellectual people! It is not a subject that lends itself well to psychological theory, but practical experience has shown me that intuitive dreams are very real and by no means infrequent.

Can two people be involved in the same dreaming process, and experience the same dream? You may discover that this does occasionally happen. The inner feelings are aware of far more than their own immediate contents, and as you will discover when you pay serious attention to your dreams and those of your family, the so-called 'collective intelligence' can control the outcome and imagery of dreams for the benefit of more than one person at once. You may sometimes dream of someone else's experiences in accurate detail, particularly when there is some sort of emotional link between you and this other person. You may also dream of another person's hopes and fears, particularly perhaps their worries and upsets, for these are more easily shared than pleasant experiences. Dream inter-reaction depends to a great extent upon the capacity to have sympathy, to empathise with and feel compassion for the other person.

Dreams of the Future

Quite a few people long to be able to dream of the future, but this is not something to aim at. Dreams of the future happen quite frequently, but they are not to be controlled. They must come about not through the will, or the ego, but from the inner feelings, simply because this is the psychic compartment in us which has the ability to see ahead. These inner feelings work beneath the surface of awareness and normally remain there, and they are completely independent of the everyday heart and mind: they cannot be directed by the will. When people use their desires to try to 'conjure up' a dream giving them the answer to some problem, the result is likely to be a wish-fulfilment dream which is really no more than the exercise of imagination.

True dreams of the future, when they happen, are quite involuntary and almost always relate to wholly private matters divulged to the dreamer alone. When you experience a dream of this sort within the family environment, you may need to keep the matter to yourself to prevent hurt feelings or worse. Intuitional dreams of the future are not really concerned with world events, unless these will affect the dreamer personally. The case is similar with 'warning dreams'. There always seems to be something desirable about dreams that deliver a timely warning, and many people long to experience them, even trying to induce them, or make themselves believe that their everyday dreams are warning them about future events. But true warning dreams are usually very private and personal, involving family and friends, and relating to matters of personal concern. The inner feelings are not normally concerned with general events, however important they may seem: they are concerned with personal psychic growth, and are not interested in 'proving themselves' and showing how clever they are by producing amazing results or forecasting events of international significance. So of course you can *try* to dream of the future; many people do, but you will probably be disappointed with the results.

CHAPTER FOUR

Moods and Emotions

The Spirit of Your Dream

IT MAY BE DIFFICULT to remember the actual emotions you were feeling as you experienced a dream, when it was actually taking place, but you are sure to remember how the memory of the dream made you feel when you woke up. You will certainly have felt the emotional atmosphere, or what has been called the 'spirit' of the dream. This can be very important in helping you to interpret the dream accurately. It will give you the 'flavour' of the way in which it is to be understood. It often happens that the theme mood changes during the course of the dream and if you can remember this it will help greatly in your interpretation: concern perhaps may have given way to reassurance or relief, suggesting that a solution to some problem is being portrayed. These are some of the feelings you are liable to recall most strongly:

Acceptance

If the dream mood seemed to be one of resignation or acceptance, it shows that you can trust the dream and put your faith in its message. It is pointing to a positive message which has already been accepted by your inner feelings, but probably not yet by your everyday, outer feelings. Try to analyse the dream in the usual way, bearing this mood in mind. Have reliance on whatever conclusion you reach, for it probably has something very valuable to convey. Try to look on the dream-source as something higher than your own conscious awareness, and accept it as an unknown place from which wisdom is to be gleaned. This will mainly apply to a personal dream rather than one related to you by a family member.

Affection

If the contents of your dream seem to have called for a mood of affection: a pleasant dream of family and friends, perhaps, this emotion is likely to be merely reflecting your own waking feelings. Sometimes, however, you may experience a powerful feeling of affection during the dream or after you wake, when the actual subject matter of the dream has been far from pleasant. This is when you should sit up and take notice. To dream of feeling affection for something you or other people may find repugnant in waking life is a clear warning that you are harbouring or hanging on to some features or characteristics which set you at odds with other people, and which you would be better off without.

Aggression

In a dream the feeling of aggression tends to suggest a psychic imbalance or an unrealistic conflict on the part of the dreamer. The first part of a complicated dream may have aggression as its theme; the second part perhaps may display a feeling of reconciliation or contentment. If the feeling of aggression persists, it may be pointing to feelings of guilt in the dreamer. Aggression in real life is also a way of discouraging an unwanted person or their unwelcome advances; shy people are often aggressive as a defensive way of hiding their shyness. In the language of dreams the mood is probably pointing to something, some characteristic, that the dreamer does not want to face up to in waking life.

Amusement

Amusement often features in children's dreams. In the case of most adults, however, a genuine feeling of amusement is rather unusual in a dream, because (as I have so often said before), the function of dreams is to instruct rather than entertain. Amusement may well, however, occur during a balancing dream as described in the previous chapter, and the purpose of this feeling will probably be to point out that you have been taking some situation or incident too seriously. Real amusement is more likely to feature in a 'wish fulfilment' dream, or a lucid dream in which the dreamer realises that he or she is dreaming, and is actually manipulating the dream events.

Apprehension

The sense of being vaguely uneasy is a very commonly experienced dream emotion that probably relates to some unsolved problem or deep-seated worry in real life. Feelings of apprehension or doubt during the course of a dream are liable to change to relief or reassurance. When this happens, you can be sure that analysis of the dream will indicate that a solution to whatever is troubling the dreamer is being suggested. Feelings of apprehension or anxiety are typical of dreams in which the dreamer seems to have become lost (you will find this category in chapter six), and they will certainly be reflecting real anxieties which may be hidden deep within the dreamer's psyche.

Arrogance

This is a thoroughly unpleasant emotion, either when awake or when dreaming – the feeling of being contemptuously superior to other people, for whatever reason. The dream in which arrogance is the over-riding theme may reflect a mistaken attitude adopted by the dreamer in waking life. You or the dreamer may not be an arrogant person in real life, but the dream may be telling you that you need to cultivate more self-confidence, that you suffer from unnecessary feelings of inferiority in your everyday dealings with others. Such feelings often feature in Adlerian dreams (see chapter five) orientated towards the pursuit of power – and seeking power amounts to much the same thing as habitually feeling inferior.

Dreams of this sensitive type need analysing very tactfully.

Concern

This is one of the major theme moods featuring in what are probably the most commonly experienced types of dream. 'Concern' dreams express exactly what they say: concern over some situation, caring deeply about some state of affairs that is not going exactly to plan, general anxiety, or a period of doubts concerning the future that the dreamer is going through. Such a dream may well relate not to the dreamer personally, but to a family member, or someone close to the dreamer emotionally, when there are some worries about that person. A 'concern' dream may act as a trigger for the dreamer to take appropriate action to improve the situation, but a dream of this nature will probably not in itself offer any solution to whatever the real-life trouble may be. When a dream has been vivid enough for the emotion to seem very important however, you may also recall whether the mood of the dream changed towards the end – concern giving way to relief or hope, or joy – because this will show when some plain solution to the problem seemed to be emerging.

Contempt

Whether in a dream or in waking life, this is a highly unpleasant negative emotion, whether that contempt was felt about certain people or about some situation. If the feeling persists after waking, the dream needs thinking through very carefully. It may be advising you to be more broad minded in your dealings with others. Even if it seems well justified, whether in a dream incident or in real life, the person who shows contempt is also behaving in a contemptible way because he or she seems to be feeling 'holier than thou'. Sometimes in a dream the attitude of contempt is being directed by other dream characters towards the dreamer. This will be a clear warning to make an effort to see matters from the others' point of view. Your analysis of the dream should make clear the real-life situation that has triggered this dream.

Despair

A feeling that 'things are getting on top of you', a sense of hopelessness; if this is the theme of your dream, the prevailing mood, you will of course interpret all the features and events of the dream in that light. If there are no recognizable features other than this feeling of despair and emptiness, and you are giving vent to these feelings in the dream, it could be acting as a catharsis for all your negative feelings which have been building themselves up – a release of pent-up emotions. In much the same vein, if you are merely experiencing these emotions in real life without actually expressing them, the dream could be advising you to be more open about releasing your emotions during your waking life. There are all sorts of reasons for feeling despair in this way. Quite often it happens that you, or anyone, may not feel able to achieve your full potential in everyday life, and with frustration after frustration you have been bottling things up enough to cause psychological problems. Because they are released, sorrows which are expressed freely are not so damaging to your psyche as those which are suffered in silence.

Distrust

Suspicion can be a useful sentiment, warning us of possible dangers, and the feeling of distrust that may permeate your dream is doing just that – warning you to take care. Plainly, all the dream details need noting and thinking round very carefully. It may be that a situation which seems normal and everyday may be misleading you in some way. There may be an element of 'the adversary' or even an assailant in the dream. If you feel some unknown person is trying to cheat you within your own dream story, you can take it as a very real warning that you need to take great care in any future dealings. If the person you distrust in the dream is a real person known to you, you will be better placed to deal with the problem. Sometimes, however, the feeling of distrust in a dream may give way to relief and acceptance, suggesting that you may have been worrying unnecessarily in real life.

Doubt

The feeling of uncertainty running through your dream, if it features a real-life recognizable situation, is reflecting the good advice to proceed with great caution. If the dream is plainly about a non-real situation, particularly if it features travelling or wishing to travel but being impeded, it implies that you have reached a crossroads in your life, whether physical, mental, emotional, or spiritual (look up 'crossroads' in chapter six). It sometimes happens that a feeling of doubt during the early part of a dream changes to a sense of relief or release, and the dream content needs recalling carefully, because there will be good advice hidden there waiting for you to find.

Exasperation

In real life when we become exasperated at some person or situation, it is usually because we have been expecting too much of them and are being unrealistic. People are as they are, and if they annoy you it might be best to avoid the sort of situation where confrontation will ensue. The situation is the same in dreams, and the implication is that you have been expecting too much of whatever or whoever you are finding exasperating. The dream may be telling you to be more broad minded and easygoing. It is no use trying to control other people's lives.

Fearfulness

A dream during which you experience fear is not really the same as a nightmare (see the previous chapter), and fearfulness is not really the same as fear itself. You are fearful lest something might happen, that some feared outcome should ensue, that a situation might become dangerous. The dream may reflect a real-life situation which you recognize, but if not, it may be telling you to have more confidence in your own ability to deal with crises as they may arise. If you have a guilty conscience and justifiably feel concerned lest your guilt should become known, this dream may well be an admonishment. The hidden inner feelings will let you know by way of dreams if you need to do something to assuage your feelings of guilt. If you have genuine concerns in real life, examine your dream very carefully for helpful clues.

Guilt

The inner self is the seat of conscience, and your own inner feelings, as the higher emotional centre of the psyche, take matters of conscience very seriously, and reflect any shortcomings in this direction as a feeling of guilt felt during your dream, or as soon as you wake. Anything you do during the day which is not really fair, anything worthy of blame, anything carrying feelings of guilt which you did not want to face up to during waking hours – all these things may have been pushed away by the conscious mind and disowned, but as we now realise, they do not simply disappear. They filter down into the receptacle of the personal unconscious mind (see the next chapter), eventually to be re-presented in the form of a dream. However disguised the dream may be, whether it seems to make sense or not to your waking mind, it is sure to carry with it an unpleasant feeling of guilt or remorse. It is always best to say 'sorry', if not to another person, at least to yourself!

Hate

Whatever the subject matter of your dream, if the feeling of hatred accompanied it and stayed with you as you woke, it can represent a call for action on your part. Equal urgency is called for if you are interpreting another family member's dream. Hate is a totally negative emotion which really has no legitimate place in the mind of a reasonable person. In a dream, whether the hatred is yours and directed towards somebody else, or whether other dream characters are projecting this unpleasantness at you, the root of it probably lies in your own or the dreamer's own conscience. The inner feelings are the seat of conscience, and the hatred you feel is expressing a deep feeling of guilt on your own part. If you really do feel hatred towards another person, try to see life from their point of view. You may find that the hate has turned to sympathy.

Helplessness

A feeling of helplessness pervading your dream usually relates to your own recent experiences. It could be called an Adlerian dream (see chapter five), reflecting a search for power or a hankering after greater confidence, and this will be the result of unfortunate real-life experiences. The dream needs searching carefully to see if it offers any clues as to the best way forward.

Horror

This powerful emotion is not really the same as fear, and when it forms the background to your dream, or remains with you after you wake, it implies that you are aghast at what you have experienced. There are horror stories and horror movies which can affect anyone who watches them, but the horror in these cases arises from some imaginative situation outside of your own psyche; you are letting it in and experiencing it. But in a dream, the chances are that the horror you feel arises from inside of yourself: from the personal unconscious mind. It will have arisen because of factors that you did not want to deal with while you were awake, perhaps matters that you refused even to consider. However, If there are real unpleasant circumstances in your life that will not leave you alone even when you sleep, study the details of the dream carefully. They may contain a clue about the best course of action for you to take. All this of course applies equally if the dreamer was a spouse or child or parent, but in their case the horrifying circumstances need uncovering very tactfully.

Joy

It would be a pleasant dream indeed that is characterized by the feeling of joy, but this is not really a normal situation. The 'great' dreams of spiritual significance, which are rare indeed, might be thought of as featuring great joy, but in fact they are far more likely to be characterised by the feeling of patience and submission rather than joy. A wish-fulfilment dream (see the previous chapter) may create the joy of achievement, but the feeling will probably be short-lived. It sometimes happens that one awakes with a feeling similar to joy, after having a dream which, on reflection, has been about rather unpleasant things and unwelcome characteristics. This could be because the dreamer has been taking a perverse pleasure in matters that he or she would be better off without.

Laughter

Laughter often features in children's dreams which are full of fun and exuberance, particularly when the child is no older than six or seven. But laughter in a dream is rarely to be experienced as an adult. In fact, there often seems to be something rather unpleasant about dream laughter, as it is usually directed against someone – and that someone may very likely be yourself In this case it will probably be reflecting the fact that you feel you have made a fool of yourself in some way during your waking life. For adults, I maintain, the purpose of dreaming is to instruct rather than to entertain, and you need to study the contents of such a dream very conscientiously.

Love

There are of course lots of different kinds of 'love', and lots of different ways of feeling and expressing it: there is sexual lust which could be called 'love'; there are close bonds of affection, and family or parental love such as a mother might feel for her child; and there is spiritual love which overrides personal feelings. Any powerful feeling of love recalled as characterising a dream, or which lingers after waking, drops an equally powerful hint as to the nature and purpose of the dream. Anyone else can analyse the dream and guess at its purpose, but only the dreamer personally is really able to interpret it.

Painful Duty

You may awake from a dream with the feeling of having done your duty, however unpleasant, a feeling uncomfortably close to self righteousness. It could be rather like a parent punishing their child and saying 'this hurts me more than it hurts you!' Your inner feelings could be dropping you the hint that you are becoming too involved in the concept of morality and losing sight of the all-important qualities of empathy, sympathy and compassion. The inner feelings themselves are concerned with morality in the sense of avoiding guilt, particularly in avoiding causing harm or discomfort to others, because all people are psychically linked on the level of these inner feelings. Don't forget that the inner feelings are also rightly known as the *higher* emotional centre; never think of them as *less* important than your ordinary, everyday feelings. They can never be accused of behaving like Mrs Grundy. But what they *can* be critical of by way of dreams is the sort of 'man-made morality' that can and often does cause harm and discomfort to others quite unnecessarily. Whatever the dream involved, the 'painful' details need to be analysed with all this in mind.

Pity

This is not a very pleasant feeling; it is rather too close to 'contempt', and implies a feeling of superiority over whoever may be the object of pity and the subject of the dream. Arrogance is something we should all strive to avoid, and nobody likes to feel 'pitied'. When this feeling colours your dream, you need to take very careful stock of all the dream details. Who or what is being pitied? If it is a real person known to you, a little self-criticism is called for. If you are pitying a complete stranger, could this 'stranger' be an unrecognised part of yourself? Study the archetypes of the unconscious mind mentioned in chapter five, and decide if you are trying to reject, or belittle, or criticise your own intuitive capacity. Your own intuition may be warning you against some conscious decision which you have recently made.

Puzzlement

There are so many of life's situations which are puzzling – any unsolved problem, in fact. In the dream being analysed, the symbolism may seem to show a completely different puzzling circumstance, rather like a cartoon. But very often the mood of puzzlement can change during the course of a dream as a solution to whatever it is that is worrying you emerges. If you can recapture the moment when this occurs and analyse the symbols playing their part at that moment, you will be well on the way to understanding the true meaning of the dream.

Sadness

The feeling of sadness remembered as typifying a dream, or that you may feel after you wake, is often associated with intuitive dreams of other lives, or so-called reincarnation dreams. In either of these cases the chances are that you will have experienced at first hand the genuine feelings of another person during whatever traumatic incident chanced to transfer itself to your own dreaming awareness. In any other type of dream, however, sadness may be associated with feelings of guilt, or it may perhaps be a genuine feeling of grief at something you have recently experienced, or some sad childhood experience which a trigger event has brought back to you. If the sense of sadness is related to some long past event, when you were unable to express grief at the time, it may be that the time has arrived to clear it out of your system.

Tearfulness

Sorrow as the background to a dream is usually referring to a psychological block - a refusal on the dreamer's part to accept his or her own contents. Could it be that you, the dreamer, are 'in denial'? We each have our own nature, our own unique inheritance giving us a basic character over which we have no control. When we feel that our 'true nature' is less than acceptable we may try to hide it. We may unconsciously strengthen our persona (see chapter five) at the expense of truth, forever putting on a false front and living a lie in case others think badly of us. There is an ancient saying: *In vino veritas*, which does not only apply to alcohol; it implies that when we drop our guard or lose our inhibitions we may be seen without our habitual disguise. The inner feelings, you may discover, have no inhibitions, and see things as they really are; in sleep we drop our guard and allow the inner feelings to take over. The dream may be pointing out your own hidden nature.

Terror

The dream you are analysing may not seem to have been about frightening things; it may appear to have been an apparently ordinary relationship dream, but you wake in a cold sweat, feeling terrified. The dream details should give you the clue: If it is not your personal dream but that of a family member, you will have a fair idea of what could have triggered it, but only the dreamer personally can know all the facts leading up to the dream, and the personal problems that prompted it. There may be a good reason why somebody wants and needs to keep something private – but when unexplained terror rears its head in your own dream, it may be that there is something you don't want the other characters in your dream to find out about. Can you identify those characters?

Worry

Quite distinct from a 'worrying dream' touched upon in the previous chapter, worry as a theme mood, particularly when it persists for some time after waking, is normally associated with an imbalance of inner contents, the negative outweighing the positive. The dream will probably display elements of Jung's shadow (see chapter five), and will need interpreting very thoughtfully. Worry invariably ensues when a person, for whatever reason, finds himself or herself unable to follow his or her own inner contents, their true character, whether this is 'good' or 'bad'. They may be to a certain extent 'living a lie', and this state of affairs in real life can be the cause of deep depression.

CHAPTER FIVE

Dream Psychology

The Self

WHO EXACTLY IS THIS PERSON you call 'me', who exactly are you, yourself? It seems a fairly elementary, not to say silly question. But in dream life things are not always as simple as they seem. In dreams it is possible to stand back and observe yourself, and you may have many different guises. If you dream of some mysterious person, it may be you, yourself. You may dream of yourself with your normal, everyday appearance; but in normal everyday life you only know yourself as you are now, and in memory as you were in the past. In dreams you may see yourself not only as you are now and in the past, but even in the future. You may see yourself dressed up in various unfamiliar ways, or naked and unashamed in public (that's you without your 'social disguise').

You may dream of yourself flying, because your inner feelings do not feel themselves to be bound to the earth like your everyday emotions; they are free from inhibitions. Or you may see yourself floundering in the mud, and very much earth-bound; your body and your personality are not so free as the inner feelings and cannot escape the influence of the earth, the pull of gravity, the rules of society. This dreaming ability to see yourself symbolised in various ways gives you a chance to see yourself and your actions objectively. It is not always easy to be honest with yourself, but in dreams that is exactly what happens. Dream images are true images, but they are portrayed in cryptic, symbolic form: they are there to be understood if you want to know the truth about yourself, but will continue to keep your true characteristics and psychic contents hidden beneath a disguise if that is what you prefer.

You may have noticed by now that, even when dreams are obviously dealing with everyday events and your relationships at home or at work or play, their prime concern is *you* and your own psychic contents. This is not to say that studying dreams makes you selfish or self-concerned, not at all, but I do maintain that the dreaming process is working to make you as an individual a better, more rounded, more complete person. It is easy to overlook this when trying to analyse and interpret your family's dreams. Loving parents are apt to overlook the obvious fact that their children are individual, independent people in their own right and not merely extensions of their parents' personalities. So when you dream of an innocent child, a baby perhaps lying on a blanket, watching and chuckling at the world, and you assume the dream is showing you your own child, it may in fact be referring your own innocent self: yourself, without the trappings of personality and all the characteristics you have acquired over the years.

In dreams you may become aware that a baby or young child has emerged from the vast sea of the collective unconscious mind (page 74), and is innocently watching everything that goes on in the world. This child is most likely to represent yourself. All the collective experiences of humankind will have become focused into one point of awareness, and that point of awareness is you! Take full advantage of the opportunity to watch and learn. If you dream of your children, you will probably see them as they normally look, and whatever they do in the dream will reflect their everyday actions, symbolically represented for you to interpret.

There are numerous ways in which the self may be depicted in dreams. Whereas the innocent child represents you without any acquired characteristics, each of these characteristics in dreams may appear as a separate person, a personification of that particular feature. Your heart, or the seat of your emotions, often takes human form in a dream. Any one of your desires or passions may be seen as independent people each with a mind of their own! People are quite often represented in dream symbolism as buildings, and you may even see yourself in the guise of a house, perhaps a great mansion, with numerous servants who may be undisciplined and neglectful. Downstairs in the basement various miscreants and mysterious beings may be lurking, while the master or mistress of the house may be somewhere upstairs in the study or the boudoir, unaware of the chaos that reigns in the house. Then again, the self may be seen as a farm where all sorts of possibilities are reared and nurtured. Or again, the self may be seen as a design formed in any number of ways, a mandala in the shape of a square or a circle. In your dream you may be symbolised by a flower – perhaps a water lily floating on a pond.

All this is another reminder that when you begin to record and understand your dreams, they will almost all seem to be centred around you, and your own unconscious contents. This may seem selfish or self-centred, but you can only begin to understand others – including your own children – when you start to understand yourself, and of course it has often been said that you cannot even begin to change the world until you have first changed yourself, and that change has to come from within.

The Personal Unconscious Mind

The study of dreams, I believe, is the very best approach to understanding the principles of the personal unconscious mind, what it is and how it works. I suppose everyone has an idea of the 'subconscious', where unremembered thoughts and impulses lurk, ready to pop up again at odd moments. The theory of the unconscious mind takes the principle a stage further. It has to be called a 'theory', I suppose, because it cannot be seen or demonstrated as a solid fact in the way that 'the brain' can be seen and demonstrated. But when you study the principles involved, you will see that it has to be so. Early psychologists first expounded the existence of this unconscious mind, at a time when people in general considered the very notion of a 'mind' that remains unconscious, as a contradiction in terms. The term 'subconscious' implies something beneath the normal conscious mind, something smaller and less important. The 'subconscious' comes to the surface when people behave in a way that is out of character, usually unpleasant; mob violence perhaps, and those little lapses that are called 'Freudian slips'.

The 'unconscious mind' is vastly more important than this. Freud may have been the first to formulate it, but it was Jung who divided the concept between the 'personal unconscious' and the 'collective unconscious' minds. Referring back to diagram 1 you will see how the personal unconscious works in a continually cycling movement, the conscious thoughts and impressions of the waking day sinking down into the dark world of the unconscious mind, where they are received and worked over by the hidden inner feelings, to be pushed back into awareness in the form of dreams and visions, waking thoughts and sudden inspirations; or, if these things are too unpleasant to be contemplated, they may be drawn down as though by gravity into the deepest and darkest part of the personal unconscious, where they remain in the form of the shadow.

The Collective Unconscious

As its name implies, while the personal unconscious mind works in relation to the individual, the collective unconscious mind acts as the 'subconscious' receptacle for the whole human race, and contains impressions, lessons to be learnt, wisdom which has been acquired by people since human reckoning began. It was Sigmund Freud who first formulated the theory of the unconscious mind as a part of the psyche that retains material forgotten or disowned by the conscious, aware mind. Carl Gustav Jung took the matter much further by separating the ideas of the personal unconscious mind from the collective unconscious. The personal unconscious mind is just that – it contains material pertaining to the individual person.

The collective unconscious mind contains material of a similar nature but common to the whole of humanity. It is from this vast sea of unconscious material that the archetypes of the unconscious mind (later in this chapter) may emerge and take on a personal identity, one that relates to the individual. It is by way of these archetypes operating through the inner feelings that the personal unconscious mind is able to link up with the collective unconscious and draw wisdom from it. For our everyday dreams of relationships and personal behaviour, the inner feelings draw the images and scenes familiar in our dreams exclusively from the personal unconscious; but when we are fortunate enough to experience a great dream, far more vivid and meaningful than ordinary relationship dreams, the inner feelings will have selected the images and symbols from the collective unconscious mind itself.

The Shadow

Sigmund Freud wrote of the *id* – the dark side of ourselves – as opposed to the *super-ego*, which is our conscientious side. When discussing dreams I prefer to use Carl Gustav Jung's term, the *shadow*, as representing the dark part of ourselves which has become repressed and hidden beneath the Inner feelings.

The best way to think of our dreams, in my opinion, is to consider them the outcome of a continuous cycling process, with all the thoughts and feelings that have come to you each day sinking down into the darkness of the unconscious mind when you go to sleep, to re-emerge in a new and modified form. If we try to understand these reassembled dream thoughts and emotions and accept that they are able to give us a true picture of our own psychic contents presented in symbolic form, we will gain some idea of the unconscious processes at work within our own mind. Anything that we have found too unpleasant for whatever reason to accept, anything we 'don't want to know about', worrying thoughts, feelings, ideas, observations, experiences, we tend to push all these away, along with all those experiences we *are* willing to accept, good and bad all mixed together. It is the job of the inner feelings to sort through them. And if they are too difficult or simply too horrendous for the inner feelings to deal with, to process and re-present in a more acceptable form, they remain there, sinking as though by the force of gravity into the lowest and darkest part of the unconscious mind.

This is the source of what are usually called nightmares (make a distinction here between the popular idea of a 'nightmare' and the medical condition mentioned in chapter three), for sooner or later these unpleasant contents are liable to force their way out, forcing their attention on the conscious mind by taking on a symbolic form – as monsters, demons, witches, the devil – the personification of anything, in fact, that the dreamer detests. When the shadow takes part in a dream, the dreamer on waking will probably fail to recognise this unpleasant apparition as his or her own, and it can indeed be very frightening indeed. But it is one of those things about which we say: 'better out than in!' When we pay attention to our dreams and accept the bad as well as the good as our own and part of ourselves, these dark contents can be evicted, bit by bit, never to return.

In Robert Louis Stevenson's famous story, *The Strange Case of Dr Jekyll and Mr Hyde,* which he said had been inspired by one of his own dreams, Stevenson visualised this unpleasant side of the personality as Mr Hyde, coming to life in the night, taking on a body, mind and personality of its own, and taking over control from the good Dr Jekyll. Of course, this is a somewhat wild stretch of the imagination, but when the shadow within the personal unconscious mind becomes too burdensome, it may balance out the image of ourselves which we like other people to see – our persona or social mask – and our dreams are then liable to alternate between the two extremes of Freud's *id* and *super-ego*: selfish attention-seeking on the one hand, and inflation or self-importance on the other, and these will be wildly conflicting dreams which defy analysis. If a sequence of this sort is proving an anxiety in your own or a member of your family's dreams, it might be a good idea to seek a new balance favouring neither one extreme nor the other. This can be done by quietening the thoughts and emotions immediately before sleeping, and adopting an attitude of 'submissive expectation': a quiet feeling of 'may the dream come as it will!' This should have the effect of broadening the possibilities of your dreams, and make them less personal.

Freudian Dreams

Sigmund Freud (1856–1939) was the pioneer psychoanalyst who first explored the unconscious mind, and who realized that the interpretation of dreams is what he called 'the royal road to knowledge of the unconscious activities of the mind'. He realized that only the individual can truly explore the recesses of his or her own unconscious mind, and that exploration of this nature can bring about a new dimension of life, release from inhibitions, and a new-found confidence. Freud seemed to be somewhat obsessed by the sexual content of dreams, and with good reason. Nowadays as a rule people's sexual lives and inclinations are very much in the open, but in Freud's lifetime this was not the case; sex was a 'closed book'. Because of this social taboo, people in western society at least tended to possess a larger, darker shadow in those Victorian, Edwardian and Georgian days than is the usual case nowadays. Sexual desires tended to be suppressed and consequently repressed – that is, driven from the conscious awareness into the dark recesses of the personal unconscious mind. Because of this Freud saw dreams as primarily sexual by nature, but presented in a disguised form so that the dreamer would not find them too upsetting or embarrassing. The actual contents of dreams he divided into two categories: the manifest, and the latent, and this is obviously just as true today as then. The manifest contents set the scene of the dream in a way anyone can understand; the latent contents contain the true meaning of the dream in a cryptic form.

To explain the process by which the content of dreams (and in particular, the sexual content) become converted into symbols, to emerge in due course as dreams, Sigmund Freud formulated the idea that we each had a built-in censor whose function it was to disguise the form of anything which the conscious mind found distasteful. He termed this the 'endo-psychic censor', visualising it as a psychic force able to modify anything incompatible with the dreamer's conscious self-opinion. In effect it was able to produce a cartoon picture out of a real situation, taking all those matters which had been rejected by the conscious mind, making them less offensive and thus more acceptable to the waking mind. You can understand the significance of a political cartoon only if you know something about the people and events to which it refers, otherwise it will remain merely an amusing drawing. He had noticed that a person might relate a dream without realizing its true meaning, and find it trivial or amusing. They, of course, were seeing the 'cartoon' without understanding its significance. When they came to understand the true meaning of the cartoon, however, the true meaning of the dream, they were liable to feel utterly mortified because it showed them as they really were: it was perhaps showing some side of themselves, their secret thoughts, feelings and actions, of which they might well have been ashamed, and which their conscious minds had tried desperately to hide. And so the purpose of the endo-psychic centre, he claimed, was to allow the dreamer to find some relief from repressed matters that had become troublesome, without causing too much distress to the waking mind. It also showed, and still shows, that if you wish to keep your thoughts secret, it is best to interpret your own dreams! Certainly a 'censoring' process is at work, now as then, though nowadays we place less importance on the sexual content: dreams take on this 'cartoon' form whether sex is involved or not. Rightly or wrongly, any dream with a disguised sexual content is often called a 'Freudian dream'.

Adlerian Dreams

As opposed to Freudian and Jungian dreams, Adlerian dreams are orientated towards power, or the sense of striving after power – or equally, towards an awareness of weakness and the absence of power. Alfred Adler (1870–1937) was a colleague of Freud, and it was he who introduced the concept of the inferiority complex. He pointed out that children during the first few years of life, being small and weak and ignorant about the ways of the world, are bound to suffer from feelings of inadequacy. The resultant sense of inferiority he saw as the root of neurosis, and the chief trigger for many of our dreams. He argued that an individual is bound to look for ways to redress the power balance, whether consciously or unconsciously, if not through their patterns of behaviour while awake, at least through their imagination by way of dreams. Dreams, he maintained, can form a source of emotional compensation, rehearsing ways to assert power in one form or another.

Bullying or being bullied are unfortunately commonplace in any child's life, and Adler went some way towards explaining why this is so. The need to dominate others rises from this childish sense of helplessness. Like a plant struggling to grow in difficult conditions, in competition with other plants, a child will dream of power and success, even if this means hurting others – like a plant smothering another plant and sprawling over it to reach the light. It is a natural situation. Dreams which include a feeling of helplessness, or of trying to gain access to a more secure place, or of dominating or bullying other people, or of being in command – these are typical Adlerian dreams. The analogy between people (and children in particular) feeling inadequate, and plants struggling for a place in the sun, is made clearer by the concept of the 'world dream', in the next chapter. There is one consolation to be found in dreams of this nature – they can be seen as representing a psychic step above the more usual dreams of everyday relationships and material ambitions; in this way an 'Adlerian dream' implies that the dreaming cycle is already well under way.

If you could say that ordinary material dreams about everyday relationships and happenings, are related to the solid background of us all, like the rock and minerals, of the earth itself, and by the same token, that 'Adlerian dreams' are related to the life of plants which are constantly striving to attain a better hold on the earth; and if you could say that 'Freudian dreams', by reflecting the sexual conflicts that we may experience from time to time, are related to the animal nature of life on earth, it will follow that 'Jungian dreams' represent a great leap forward from these categories, because they relate entirely to ourselves, to our inner selves, to the life force that rightfully belongs to human beings.

Jungian Dreams

Carl Gustav Jung (1875–1961) was interested in the psychological process which he called 'individuation'. This involved exactly that process which I have described as the cycle of the dreaming self: a gathering into the self of collective factors common to the whole of humankind, and assimilating into consciousness that part of the psyche which is normally unconscious. He divided people into various 'types' according to which psychic function they used the most: intellectual, emotional, physical, and whether they were introverted or extroverted. Everyone is a combination of all these things in various proportion, establishing exactly what sort of people we are. Most importantly, he formulated the existence and described the characteristics of the various archetypes of the unconscious mind (opposite), which are manifestations of collective factors common to all mankind, coming to individual awareness and modified to fit each individual.

Any dreams which feature these archetypes, often invoking the higher intuitive powers of the psyche, as well as dreams which contain material that seems to have arisen from non-personal or collective sources, could be called Jungian dreams. Whilst describing the characteristics of archetypes which come to awareness by way of dreams, Jung encouraged the people who consulted him to analyse and interpret their own dreams. He ascribed great importance to the keeping of accurate dream records, and also to making drawings or paintings to bring out their meanings while still fresh in the memory. Even in the case of bafflingly complicated or obscure dreams, he said: ' If we meditate on a dream sufficiently long and thoroughly – if we take it about with us and turn it over and over – something almost always comes of it'.

Archetypes

The concept of the archetype was formulated by the famous pioneer psychiatrist Professor Jung, and expressed in his system of analytical psychology. Jung could see a tendency common to all people, to understand and regulate their lives in a way conditioned by the whole previous history of humankind. This tendency involved a series of shared experiences which grouped various aspects of their collective psyche into recognisable forms intuitively understood. These primordial images remained basically constant, though in their form and detail they could vary widely to suit the individual's understanding and cultural background. These subtle manifestations of intuitive perception rose to awareness and made their presence known mainly by way of dreams, particularly when something momentous or awe-inspiring was taking place, and perhaps even more importantly, whenever a change came about or was due to come about in an individual's psychological orientation.

Whether we call them 'bundles of psychic energy', or emotional constants on which people pin their faith, in our dreams these archetypal images come to our awareness to warn, or advise, or admonish, or reassure us. When this happens, we just 'know' they are trustworthy and usually feel duty-bound to take heed of their messages. They leave a lasting impression on our minds, so that we are left in no doubt as to their psychic reality, their sincerity of purpose. Though they usually remain below our surface of awareness, they could be called collectively the highest part, the pinnacle, of our own individual selfhood. Because they are shared in common with the rest of humanity and originate from the sum total of human history, in the advice they offer they carry the strength and weight of all human wisdom and experience.

The *self* may frequently appear as a dream archetype, particularly when visualised as an innocent child experiencing the world and observing our every move, looking at our actions from the point of view of complete innocence, without the hampering trappings of personality, watching that we do not act in a way harmful to ourselves. In the dreams of men and boys, there is the *anima,* and in women the *animus,* representing the feminine element, the 'female side' within a man which enables him to understand and relate to women or girls, and the male element within a woman which gives her an intuitive understanding of men or boys and their needs. In both men and women there is the archetype of the *wise person*, available to offer good advice in times of stress; there is an example of this type of wise advice from an archetype in the 'grandfather's dream' given in chapter one. The wise person often appears in the guise of a doctor, if there is a medical or psychiatric problem.

There is the archetype of the *hero* or *heroine*, ready to come to the rescue and point out a course of action in difficult times. Variations of this wise and authoritative figure are the *king* and the *queen,* the *father figure,* the *goddess* or other divine person, and though these dream figures are totally authentic and trustworthy, they may take any form drawn from the individual's experience and expectations; the collective wisdom of the whole human race focused on a single individual's needs. Then of course there is the *personal shadow* which occupies the darkest part of our own personal unconscious mind and may appear in the form of a witch or wizard, the devil, or any apparition which the dreamer finds unpleasant – and this is an archetype made wholly from the individual's own contents, fears and follies.

There is the *persona*, named after the mask which actors in ancient Greek dramas used to wear, which early psychologists likened to the 'mask' or public 'face' we like to present to the world, for matters of our own pride and self-preservation. It is rather similar to Freud's endo-psychic censor in that it conceals a person's true nature, except that the mask or persona is largely a consciously selected image. The whole personality itself could be said to consist of all the features which may well be represented by the archetype of the persona, and nakedness in a dream portrays a person without their persona, without their personality. To some people the persona is very important, to others less so. Dreams in which archetypes feature are very important, and it is usually easy to tell on waking whether a dream character referred to a real person known to you, to an anonymous bystander, or to a genuine archetype sent by your own inner feelings to help you. Though primordial and archetypal, the form and function of all these stems directly from our own life experiences, and can give us valuable information about ourselves when we heed their message.

Collective Intelligence

At the level of the inner feelings, the inner self, everything can be shared, and everything can be known about our fellows. When you take up dream analysis, and try seriously to interpret dreams for others, in all probability you will soon become aware of this amazing human capacity. It is connected with the idea of the collective unconscious: at a certain level of the psyche, a great deal may be shared in common. When you have experience of this, you may well think you have stumbled upon something truly miraculous. It never ceases to amaze me. The famous John Donne was hinting at this underlying web of communication when he wrote 'no man is an island, entire of itself'.

What I call the collective intelligence is not a belief, or a theory; it is an experience, and it is most likely to come to our awareness when we concern ourselves with the dream world. For instance, it might be that you have been reading about the dream-work of Freud, or Adler, or Jung, or some other lesser known dream-worker, and learnt about the symbols and themes and methods most familiar to them. Then if someone presents you with their dream for analysis, you will find that it corresponds with the specialist material which you happen to have read about, and with which you are now familiar. In other words, that person will have dreamed a dream not for themselves but for *you* to interpret. Similarly, their dream may contain information that is plainly intended for *you* rather than for them. Incredible coincidences in real life too, coincidences that cannot actually be 'put down to coincidence', are manifestations of the collective intelligence. Things like this can happen because all humanity, at the deep level of the inner feelings, is itself linked in a way quite unsuspected by the everyday waking mind. We can get an inkling of the truth of this when we have an intuitional experience. Jung described these things as synchronicity – happenings which are plainly related in practice, though their correspondence may have no scientific explanation. All in all, such matters hint at the miraculous world that can be uncovered when we study our own and our family's dreams.

CHAPTER SIX

Transcendent Dreams

Dream Development

ONCE YOU GET TO KNOW about the cycle of the dreaming self, and agree with me that the process of dream formation starts kicking into action as soon as you go to sleep, you will have no difficulty appreciating the way in which the dreaming process develops beneath the threshold of awareness, and builds itself up through the night. From the initial chaos of the dozing evening dreams, those dreams which start to take shape during the early part of the sleeping period will tend to be about things and places and normal everyday occurrences. Of course, you may not have regular sleeping habits, you or members of your family may for instance work nights and sleep during the day. In that case the term 'evening dream' will refer to dreams that happen soon after you fall asleep. Should you wake up soon after falling asleep the chances are that any dream in your memory will seem chaotic and meaningless. This is because the inner feelings have not yet had a chance to begin their work. As the night – or your period of sleep – progresses, remembered dreams will be that much more meaningful.

The same is true of dozing dreams: especially when you are getting on in years like me and are inclined to fall asleep sitting in your chair, you may find that you are experiencing instant dreams of a somewhat chaotic nature. Strangely enough, they will have seemed to make perfect sense whilst you were experiencing them, but as soon as you wake it becomes plain that they are quite nonsensical. This is perfectly normal; all the thoughts and impressions gained during your waking hours are still passing down into the personal unconscious mind, and have not yet been sorted and characterized by the inner feelings into a form which makes sense. Even if you can remember dreams of this nature clearly, it will probably be of little use to try to analyse them; they will still be nonsense.

Dreams occurring a little later will make more sense, and they will tend to be about normal, everyday affairs; general relationships with friends, family and colleagues. These are dreams that need analysing and interpreting carefully, because they may well contain psychological truths and useful hints, especially concerning the dreamer's relationships with other people. Some dreamers report long and complicated dreams of this nature. Nine out of ten of these 'normal' dreams will concern the experiences of the previous day. Though interesting, they will not yet have begun to delve into the deeper contents of the personal unconscious. Later in this chapter you will see that these are 'groundwork' dreams belonging to the psychic level of materiality, corresponding, you could say, with the very earth on which we live. This is no bad thing, but when you start studying and recording your dreams you are likely to experience dreams which reflect a higher or more evolved psychic level, perhaps culminating in dreams of the collective unconscious, or even the mysterious realm known as the human world of spirit.

Dreams experienced later on during the sleeping period will be less about normal relationships and more about underlying attitudes, involving in particular aggressive and competitive attitudes coming to the surface. The dreamer's inner nature is beginning to be uncovered and exposed to view! They may well reflect the impulses expressed in 'Adlerian dreams' (refer back to the previous chapter), that is, they will express the principle of establishing one's own position and status in the world. Any feelings of inadequacy, or domination, or being bullied, will feature in dreams of this category. Later still dreams may also display the spirit of competition, but they will be more 'Freudian' in nature. The instincts being uncovered in this type of dream will be based on sex and morality, and fears about outsiders intruding on the dreamer's privacy. They will be concerned more about socializing or communicating with others rather than struggling with them, and they are very likely to centre on the family and family relationships. Towards dawn, or nearing the end of the sleeping period, dreams will reflect a more constructive quality. These could quite accurately be termed 'Jungian dreams'. The 'archetypes' (see the last chapter) are likely to play a part in these dreams, which will have reached a very deep level of the personal unconscious mind. They may be less 'real' than earlier dreams, but they are the most important, in my view: they may not be particularly pleasant for the dreamer to remember, but are sure to contain good advice, and they are far more likely at this time to present solutions to any problems and worries he or she may have been experiencing in waking life.

Meditation and Morality

Different people may have very different ideas about the actual meaning of 'meditation', but to most, I suppose, the concept seems to imply some kind of quiet time, preferably spent alone. Many people nowadays, both young and old, feel that meditation is a 'good thing to do'. But there are two basic possibilities here, which are diametrically opposed to one another, and they concern one's attitude to higher matters, to non-material or spiritual possibilities. If your 'meditation' is simply aimed at finding the best course of action in some sphere or another, work or play, this is 'pondering' or 'reflecting' rather than 'meditating', and there is no harm in that. Religious or yogic meditation, on the other hand, is not really about thinking (although it probably involves strengthening the mind in some way); it is more likely to be directed towards keeping out unwanted influences, or 'rising above the influences of the world'. This is the type of meditation that I feel bound to criticise, in the light of what I have experienced and written about so far during the process of analysing and interpreting dreams.

The point is, the whole *self* has to include all influences that come into it, whether those influences are considered to be good or bad. A healthy dream life depends on the free circulation of influences within the self, and 'bad' influences should have no ill effect. Suppose someone succeeds in shutting out bad influences through religious meditation, the chances are they will have shut out good influences as well, because of course we cannot know whether something is going to be good or bad before we have become aware of it, and once we have become aware of an influence, it will already have entered the self. Don't let us fool ourselves. Some kinds of religious imagery picture the meditating self as a pure lotus flower floating on calm waters. The flower symbolises the self, and the water symbolises the personal unconscious mind. This may be an attractive image, but taken too far the practice can cut off contact with everything beneath the surface of the water – representing everything that has become trapped and held in the personal unconscious mind. When this happens the inner feelings will be unable to function in any meaningful way. Any dreams you then experience will merely be surface ego-dreams leading you nowhere.

And so meditation should be *submissive* rather than purposeful. If a member of your family thinks meditation is a good thing, ask them to look at it in relation to their dream life. The only kind of meditation that will help our dream life along (and set us on a course aimed towards psychic completion), is purely passive meditation: this consists of allowing our thoughts and emotions to subside, in full awareness; not cutting ourselves off from all the influences that surround us, but laying ourselves open to such influences as may arise from a source higher than the spiritual level of ordinary humans. On a note of caution: anything approaching a state of trance should be strictly avoided, as it will result in an unwanted and quite unnecessary invasion of influences from a source *lower* than the proper human level. You don't want to become possessed like a shaman or a voodoo practitioner; it may sound like fun, but believe me it's no joke, I'm being serious here! The secret is, sit quietly and be open to all around you.

Your conscience hurts when you break your own rules. It's really a human way of looking at your own instincts, the natural limits set out for normal human behaviour. Animals don't have a conscience because they live according to their instincts, so they have no need of such a thing. Humans lost their true instincts back in prehistoric days! The inner feelings are the seat of conscience, and questions of morality when they occur in dreams, usually relate to matters of conscience and feelings of guilt which need to be worked through. Even small matters which may be not quite honest are of concern to the inner feelings, matters which the outer feelings or everyday emotions would think unimportant and happily forget. This was a dream that brought home to the dreamer how important little matters of honesty can be:

I was in a large room lined with hundreds of different shapes of different colours. There was a narrow gap between some sort of cupboards, with some people standing around just outside. To show them how easily I could get through the narrow gap I held my arms above my head and sort of danced through. I suppose I was just showing off. Then I saw that I had touched the sides, and left a nasty stain on my dress.

This dream proved easy to analyse: the large room with the coloured items was a shop, a supermarket in symbolic form, and the narrow gap between cupboards represented the checkout point. In dreams, clothes represent the personality, and dirt or a stain on the clothes symbolise a 'stain' on the personality. In the dream she wanted to show the other customers that she was impervious to such trivial matters: and what was that trivial matter? The dream made her remember that she had been given too much change the last time she went shopping. "Well," she said. "There was a sign telling me that they could not rectify mistakes in the change after I had left the checkout, so what was I to do?" Yes, of course, that sign was meant to protect the store against minor cheats, but by keeping quiet she was robbing the checkout girl of the missing amount. Her everyday feelings may not have been bothered, but her inner feelings could not overlook this misdemeanour.

The study of dreams tells us that such minor things are liable to build themselves up and form part of the shadow if they are not recognised, accepted and resolved, and the outcome of ignoring them is to add to the burden of the personal unconscious mind in a way which may seem out of all proportion to the importance of such seemingly insignificant acts. As far as the inner feelings are concerned, the concept of 'guilt' involves acts which have affected other people in a negative way, hurting someone's feelings perhaps, diminishing them to some extent. This is not merely an altruistic way of looking at the world; it is because all people are linked on the level of the inner feelings. Whilst people still live in the soul-level of materiality such things may seem to have no significance. But once an individual begins to take the 'return journey' in spiritual terms back to their own innocent childhood, and this is exactly what happens when you begin to log and analyse your dreams, these matters become increasingly important.

Inner Submission

It is my favourite theme: dreams are produced by the inner feelings, which are part of the personal unconscious mind. In dreams this higher emotional centre of the psyche deals with all the matters which have not been finalized by the conscious mind. It reassembles them and re-presents them in the form of dreams, or images which are more acceptable to your waking mind. It is then up to you, or your conscious mind, to interpret these images and take them to heart.

The process of creating dreams cannot really be made conscious, though it can sometimes be helped along. If your everyday mind, your will-power, or your ego intrude into a dream and interfere in the selection of images, as happens sometimes during a lucid dream or in a wish-fulfilment dream, the cycling or clearing-out process will stop. The will or determination is an indispensable tool of the whole person, and we would be fairly helpless creatures without it; but it cannot be expected to deal with

90

the non-material concerns of the personal unconscious mind, and in particular any matters which arrive from a spiritual source, that is, from *above* the limits of the human capacity. Matters which are outside the capacity of our everyday mind to perceive can only be received into our awareness when the will, or the ego, is in a state of submission and has ceased to function – if only temporarily. This is what should happen during sleep. Some dream books recommend deliberately willing certain sorts of dream to happen, by concentrating on them before going to sleep, a practice known as incubating dreams.This is quite understandable in cases where a particular problem needs to be resolved, and of course it is for the individual to decide: but I personally would advise against it.

The reason for my attitude is this: there are basically three types of dream:everyday or material dreams, deeply psychological dreams involving Jung's archetypes, and spiritual dreams. When you start recording and analysing your dreams, they should progress from the material, everyday dreams of social relationships, to the deeper more personal dreams when the inner feelings begin clearing out any unwanted clutter in the personal unconscious mind, to dreams which include the collective unconscious mind, even touching on the human world of spirit. Once an individual has started along a truly spiritual path in this sense (as distinct from a religious one, or an occult one, or one involving some sort of spiritualism), his or her dreams will change their nature and leave the everyday, material dreams behind. Purifying or 'clearing out' dreams are then likely to be experienced quite frequently. Archetypes such as the doctor, the wise adviser, and the policeman, will often appear and give advice or supervise your progress. Unpleasant dream symbols such as excreta, dirt, or mud, or toilets that don't work properly, will give some idea of the weight or extent of unwanted material that has become lodged in the personal unconscious mind. Purifying dreams of this nature may seem thoroughly unpleasant, but they are being realistic in their symbolism. If we accept them with a submissive attitude they will tell us where we are on our journey through life, and what needs to be done to help us on our way.

Great Dreams

Just to recap, you will know from reading about the continuous cycle of the dreaming self and the development of dreams covered earlier in this chapter, that the formation of dreams is a cyclic process – that is, it progresses and gathers momentum throughout the sleeping period as the thoughts and feelings and sensations of the day are assimilated and worked over by the inner feelings. The longer this process lasts, the more vivid and constructive one's dreams can be expected to be. The inner feelings normally draw on the contents of the personal unconscious mind to produce dream symbols that can be presented to your conscious mind. For more vivid and meaningful dreams this higher emotional centre is able to draw on images from the vastly more extensive collective unconscious. These images stem not from your own experience alone, but from the collective experience of the whole of mankind, and dreams of this nature are most likely to be dawn dreams. Arriving just before you awake in the morning, they are particularly intended to be remembered by your everyday mind (remember the collective intelligence overseeing our progress): a dawn dream is warning you to sit up and listen, because they will be imparting information that has arisen outside of the self.

A great dream is a term used to describe dreams which contain more than the usual type of contents, cryptic or otherwise. Such dreams will certainly draw on the collective unconscious and even the mysterious spiritual world to bring the dreamer an important message. Anyone who experiences one is usually left in no doubt about its special nature. Such dreams usually occur in the early dawn, at a time just prior to waking, when they are most likely to be remembered in detail, and they are always very vivid. The nature of the message or information they bring is entirely a personal matter, though it may relate to other people as well as the dreamer personally. A study of the cycle of creation and the great world dream (page 94) will show that these dreams represent something of great significance and value to the fortunate individual who experiences them.

Cycle of Creation in Dreams

The cycle of creation is connected with the concept of the great world dream (overleaf), and equally it is connected with the cycle of the dreaming self. Every individual is constantly experiencing a personal cycle involving the conscious and the unconscious minds. This is usually an unconscious process, but it comes to awareness and becomes most apparent when we begin to record and analyse our dreams. We could say that the world itself, looked at in non-material terms, is also experiencing a continual cycle involving the actual creation and development of the planet: the rocks, sea and soil; the plants; the animals; and the humans. It is a psychic rather than a physical cycle, and every individual creature – or in this case, every human being – potentially possesses the nature of this same cycle in miniature.

Most dreams, those involving everyday affairs and relationships, could be said to be purely material dreams, equating to the basic geological structure of the earth. Dreams which show an inclination to rise above the mundane and involve something of a struggle for inner power and expansion, a growing away from the basic ground common to all, could be said to equate to the growth of plant life on the earth and the fact that plants are programmed to struggle against their competitors and claim their own place in the sun. We can say these are 'Adlerian dreams' because they reflect the psychological principle of power-seeking as expounded by Adler. Dreams which seem to be orientated towards a much broader outlook, full of fantastic imaginings, moral boundaries and intellectual efforts, could be said to equate to the animal life of the earth, with its free-ranging mobility. We can say this category includes 'Freudian dreams' because sexually orientated dreams are to be found here. Dreams which contain images from the collective unconscious and seem concerned with a yet broader perspective, or an overview of the world, could be said to equate with the life of human beings on earth. These we can say will be 'Jungian dreams', aiming as they do towards the psychological goal that Jung called individuation or complete integrity of the individual.

The next stage, dreams of the mysterious realms we call the human world of spirit, represent the culmination of the dreaming process as a means of advancement. So, looked at in this way, the great majority of our dreams can be seen to be of a material nature, dreams in which the cycle of creation is not functioning on an individual basis. If we pay attention to our dreams, record them and try to understand them, we can show willing to help this great cycle sweep us along with it, and include us in its process of psychic development. The more conscious our dream life, the more our psychic selves will be in tune with the cycle of creation.

The Great World Dream

Religions each have their own way of picturing creation and the beginning of human life, and there is no need to interfere with people's beliefs. Science, of course, has its own way of doing the same thing, and no-one will dispute scientific facts. But the world of dreams is a symbolic world. Anything that is non-material simply has to have a symbolic explanation because our brains, being of a material nature themselves, cannot encompass anything like that. And science (whatever scientists may say) has no way of approaching non-material matters because such things cannot be analysed. Science is simply not interested in anything that cannot be demonstrated or proved.

So nobody should complain when I try to explain my hypothesis of the great world dream. It has to be considered as the ever-present background to the cycle of creation, and the cycle of the dreaming self, the background to all our dreams, and indeed the background of nature itself. Think of it first in relation to the world spinning in space. Above the horizon all is bathed in light; below all is in darkness. Sunrise, or the east, is to the left. Sunset, or the west, is on the right. The cycle of creation runs in a clockwise direction, set into motion, we could say, by the archangelic section. The Archangel Lucifer, in that particular myth, fell to earth, and became custodian of the material world. And the light that came down during the 'fall of Lucifer' sparked off the cycle of creation, of constant re-creation in a never-ending cycle. The creation of the natural world begins with bare earth, the oceans of the world, and solid rock. This basic state begins first to support plant life; then animal life; and finally human life, and so the cycle should continue. Humans in this scale should evolve and develop into something we can only hint at: something 'spiritual'.

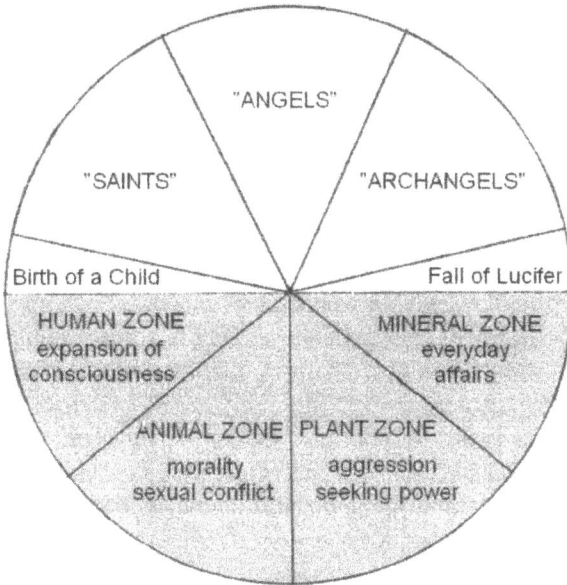

The Great World Dream

Both the myths and religions of the world tell us what actually happened to the human race. Instead of following on the cycle of creation, from minerals to plants, from plants to animals, from animals to humans, and from humans to this unknown higher state, people began to chase after all the benefits of materiality, of civilisation. And who can blame us for that. The story of creation that I was brought up with tells how Adam and Eve got themselves evicted from the Garden of Eden (that is, they lost their original submissive human instincts). All the wealth and comfort of the world is to be found in the material, mineral zone of nature. Our civilisations depend on such things as stone, metal, oil, gold and diamonds, and there were none of these in the Garden of Eden. So now any newborn child emerging from the light enters the 'human' zone and, aiming towards the benefits of civilisation available in the 'mineral' zone, is drawn down towards that goal.

Now think of this same cycle, this world dream diagram, in relation to your own self. Your conscious, thinking mind is represented by the light above the horizon. Below the horizon is your dreaming self – your personal unconscious mind. As you fall asleep, tired of all the day's happenings, your thoughts and feelings slide down into the darkness, where your inner feelings begin to create your dream life. The mineral or material zone represents your evening dreams, chaotic, like the world when it was first created, and as they settle into a firm pattern, they become the sort of dream that represents your daily affairs, everyday, 'normal' dreams. Then gradually plants begin to grow, each plant striving to establish itself, get its roots down and spread its leaves over those of its neighbours, and this, by and large, is the nature of these early dreams (remember 'Adlerian' dreams!). Then animals evolve, setting out their boundaries, competing, eating and having sex. ('Freudian' dreams relate to these animal-type dreams halfway through your sleeping period). Finally humans evolve, and your dreams at this late stage will be concerned with 'human' matters, perhaps involving images from the collective unconscious mind, and relating to 'Jungian' dreams, urging the dreamer towards what Jung called individuation – a fairly well completed psychic state in which you accept all your own unconscious contents. So, as above, so below. You will see that your dream world really does relate to the world of nature itself.

Although absolutely necessary for civilisation, materiality, materialism, is not the ideal spiritual condition for people. In spiritual terms we seem to have been travelling in the wrong direction. This, basically, is where our 'great' dreams fit in to the equation; this is the fundamental purpose of all dreams above the everyday, relationships type of dream – to get us to begin climbing back the way we came. Having reached our material goal and acquired all the benefits we need, our best plan is to link up, on the inner dimension, with the cycle of creation and start back through the world of nature to attain the truly human level again. This can only be done by way of 'inner submission' (see above). Having finally reached the point of birth and regaining the light, we will have been 'born again' in the Christian sense, and our progress from then on should be heavenwards. The best way to begin the return journey on the inner plane is to start recording and listening to our dreams. I am claiming that this is the true function of dreams. The world of nature where we live is all part of the great world dream, we are all symbols of that dream, and the great dawn dream of the world is to achieve the perfection of the human psyche. If you don't want to go along with these ideas, with this particular myth, that's fine. You don't have to teach it to your children. Call me an old fool and just forget I mentioned it.

Dreams of the Future

Quite a few people long to be able to dream of the future, but this is not really something to aim at. Dreams of the future happen surprisingly frequently, but they are not to be controlled. They must come about not through the will, or the ego, but from the inner feelings – the psychic compartment in us which has the ability to see ahead. These inner feelings cannot be coerced by the conscious mind. As you will be well aware by now, they work beneath the surface of awareness and normally remain there, completely independent of the everyday heart and mind. When people use their desires to try to 'conjure up' a dream giving them the answer to some problem, the result is likely to be a wish-fulfilment dream which is really no more than the exercise of imagination. True dreams of the future, when they happen, are quite involuntary and almost always relate to wholly private matters divulged to the dreamer alone. There is an example of this type of dream in the first chapter. Such dreams are simply not concerned with world events, unless these events will affect the dreamer personally.

Some dream books recommend trying to induce predictive dreams by concentrating on some issue, or perhaps on tomorrow's newspaper headlines, in the hope of dreaming about events to come. But *this* dream book warns against it. I think it would be a grave mistake to introduce ideas like this into your family. If we are going to dream of future events, a much higher source of intelligence than our everyday brains will decide it for us. If you succeed in doing it yourself, you will have short-circuited or disrupted the dreaming process by forcing your own ego into territory where it has no business to go. Genuine predictive dreams, certainly in my own experience, tell of events that will take place within a few days, and almost always they are personal matters which will affect the dreamer alone. They warn of events that are due to take place, so that the dreamer will be prepared for them when they arrive. They may also impart information about the lives of others, and when they do the matter should usually be kept private. Some dreams may seem to be predicting future events, when analysis will show that the prediction is symbolic and allegorical, and not to be taken literally.

So-called veridical dreams are closely allied to dreams of the future. The term applies to dreams during which you dream of previously unknown facts, incidents, places and people, all of which later turn out to be completely true, though they are often accurate in a completely symbolic way. Such dreams are also closely allied to intuitive dreams, or any dream in which the collective intelligence is involved. Veridical dreams involving other people, often family members or close friends, usually follow some traumatic incident which recently happened to the subject of the dream. In any case it implies a close emotional involvement between the subject and the dreamer. These are frequently dawn dreams, and seem to depend upon one's ability to receive them – they depend upon the principles of empathy, sympathy, and compassion being well developed on the part of the dreamer.

There seems to be something fascinating about dreams that deliver a timely warning, and many people long to experience them, even trying to induce them, or make themselves believe that their everyday dreams of relationships are warning them about future events. But I would repeat that true warning dreams are usually very private and personal, involving family and friends, and relating to matters of personal concern. The inner feelings are simply not normally concerned with general events, however important they may seem to our everyday minds; they are concerned with personal psychic growth, and are not interested in 'proving themselves' by producing amazing results or forecasting events of international significance.

A 'white lie' dream is my term for a warning dream of a personal nature that seems to bear all the hallmarks of a true warning dream, advising the dreamer to take or avoid taking certain action and giving reasons that appear to be valid – e.g., avoid travelling to an appointment as planned because an accident was due to happen along the way. After the dreamer has followed this advice in good faith, it transpires that there was no accident situation, but another far more subtle reason why they should *not* attend that particular interview. What else could that be but a 'white lie' – a deliberate untruth told with good intent. In my experience, white lies are quite acceptable not only to the inner feelings, but to the whole realm of spirit.

Occasionally a true dream of future events may occur in the form of a 'waking inspiration'. In effect the dream with all its use of symbolism will occur to your everyday, wide-awake self, going about your daily business. When this happens, for a brief while you will have become 'psychic', a seer of future events, though you will probably not realise what is happening until the actual event takes place, usually within a couple of days. It is a situation in which real-life events fall into place in symbolic terms in order to portray some particular truth or exchange an important intuitional piece of information. Dreams, of course, are normally arranged and their symbols or images selected by the inner feelings acting beneath the level of awareness. Waking dreams or inspirations are real-life situations arranged by the inner feelings when this higher emotional centre is functioning temporarily within the level of awareness. This has certainly happened to me, but the circumstances were and are so sensitive and personal that they had better remain untold. If and when this sort of thing happens to you, as a result of studying the dream lives of yourself and your family members, you will see exactly what I mean.

Dreams of Reincarnation

These are dreams in which the dreamer experiences an incident or series of incidents in the life (and often the death) of some real but usually completely unknown person who lived at some time in the past. Such dreams are normally very vivid and there is little doubt that they do feature real incidents in the lives of real people. Quite often they cross racial boundaries and involve matters about which the dreamer was previously ignorant. In this sense they are veridical dreams. Some people go to great lengths to establish that the characters and the incidents are or were genuine, and take this as proof of reincarnation. But don't forget that this life from past times belonged to another person, and not to you personally. Everyone is 'me', and every person lives their life out as a unique personality. During a 'reincarnation dream' the dreamer is certainly experiencing what that other person experienced, but we might recall the equally vivid and 'true' intuitive dreams about traumatic or unpleasant incidents in the lives of real people – who are still alive and known to the dreamer. I have personally experienced both types of dream and the principle is exactly the same in both cases. You are seeing through their eyes and feeling their emotions.

We should also be aware that on the level of the inner feelings, which of course are responsible for choosing our dream images, all people are linked: thoughts and feelings can be shared between people whose inner feelings have (to some extent) come to awareness. These dreams of others are also 'shared' in this sense, and you may find to your surprise that they always seem to involve unpleasant emotions and traumatic incidents, often involving the death or impending death of the subject or others closely associated with them. Happy incidents never seem to be remembered and transmitted in this way. To be on the receiving end of such dreams calls for sympathy and empathy, or compassion. Your desires really have nothing to do with it. Hypnotic regression is sometimes practiced in an attempt to strengthen or encourage or recapture such dreams, and there is always the risk of invoking wish-fulfilment dreams if the mind or ego plays a part in this. This is a typical 'reincarnation' dream which was experienced by a member of my own family:

I seemed to be about seventeen years of age. I and about four ladies were getting out of a horse-drawn coach. We were all expensively dressed. We were being hurried out of the coach by a man on horseback. He was very well known to us in the dream, and I remember thinking how strange it was to see him with such very muddy, dirty breeches, because he was usually immaculately dressed. We were outside a small inn, which was on the corner where two roads met. The horseman said: 'I am sorry to disturb you ladies. You will be all right, but we must have the horses.' The coach had been drawn by two horses, and another man had already taken them out of the shafts. Riding his own horse he cantered away, leading the two coach horses. Inside the inn we all gathered round a large table. An elderly couple (apparently the innkeeper and his wife) stood at one end of it. After a few moments we heard a tremendous clatter of horses, and we could see a great many men, who looked in through the window. We could see that they were Cromwell's troops. The innkeeper seemed very nervous. He grabbed his gun, which was in the corner near him, and fired blindly. I don't think he took aim. I heard a loud bang and felt myself falling, and realised I had been shot. I don't think he had actually meant to shoot me but he panicked. There was some shouted conversation between the innkeeper and his wife. She was saying something like 'Oh, the poor thing!' and he was saying something like 'Well, what could I do, they'll think we've been harbouring them!' That was the end of the dream.

Dreams of Heaven

When people dream of 'heaven' their experience seems to vary according to their own individual expectations. The point is, I think, no living person really knows what 'heaven' is like, or if they did know, they would be unable to describe it. The whole point of heaven, surely, is that such a place or condition is not dependent upon materiality. If someone has a dream of heaven, or a 'near death' experience when a person seems to have come back from the dead, they will describe their experiences. But if it is possible to describe something in material terms, then that something must have been based on materiality, and by that very token it could not really have been an experience of 'heaven'. Someone who has recently been bereaved may well dream of meeting or reuniting with their spouse in a beautiful place that they must assume to have been heaven. People often speak of entering a brilliantly lit room full of people, or of walking in a beautiful sunlit meadow full of flowers. The following is a rather typical dream following the death of the dreamer's husband:

I dreamed I was walking with my husband along a country road when it suddenly grew dark, and then became pitch black. I could no longer see him, and we got separated. I just kept calling and groping about, but to no avail, so I just kept trudging on and on through the dark. After a very long time I saw a door open, as though across the road, showing a brilliant light. Three or four people were trooping slowly in. I dashed across the road to ask them where I was, but then as I reached the door I saw my husband standing a few feet inside, so I ran in. I was so excited, I grabbed his arm and asked him: 'What are you doing here?' He said: 'I was waiting for you.' I said: 'But how did you know I'd be coming here? I was lost; I might never have found you.' He just said calmly: ' Oh, I knew you'd come.' We wandered off arm in arm, and I said: 'This is such a beautiful place, flowers everywhere, and everyone so happy.' My husband said: 'It's called the Elysian Fields.' We walked on very happily. Then I became aware that I was dreaming, and fell into a deep dreamless sleep.

If you refer back to the diagram of the world mandala (the 'Great World Dream'), earlier in the chapter, and if you like to think in abstract terms, you could well imagine that this type of 'material heaven' is situated in that light zone on the right of the diagram – a spiritual bit of materiality. But nevertheless a dream of this sort can be a great comfort to anyone who has recently been bereaved. Personally, I think that any 'true' idea of heaven would have to stem from the *left* of the diagram, the place of new birth. This would depend on the individual having followed the 'cycle of creation'; it would also depend on having acquired what I might term holistic understanding. The term implies having the ability to accept anything – a person, a situation, a dream – as a whole without attempting to analyse this or that detail. The more 'advanced' a person is in spiritual terms, or the more psychologically 'individuated' they are, the more likely will they be to accept wholes rather than look at the details. The nature of analysis is to break down 'wholes' to discover what they are made of; but in human terms the 'whole' is more than merely the sum total of parts, and the more one analyses, the less likely one is to arrive at a holistic understanding. The basic reason for this is that spiritual or non-material matters cannot be analysed, because they lie beyond the scope of the human mind. Even the cleverest scientists, you might conclude, can never arrive at a holistic understanding while they rely on their own brain-power to achieve that understanding. But as this book points out, dreams cannot be understood or interpreted with the mind if they are not first analysed for their meaning. The understanding itself has to arrive independently. Truly spiritual dreams when they are experienced will not need analysis, and this book will then no longer be needed.

CHAPTER SEVEN

Dream Symbols

Subjects and Objects

ABANDONMENT *Shedding of responsibilities*

If it is you being abandoned

This dream may of course relate clearly to some real-life incident, and if it seems to contain no answer or solution it will simply be expressing your own feelings at being let down. If there is no real-life equivalent that you can see, try to recapture the mood of your dream: who or what has abandoned you, and what was your dream situation as a result? The symbol is closely allied to the dream symbol of being lost, and may be pointing out that you have lost your way in life.

If you are abandoning something or someone else

If the dream characters are real people known to you, the meaning of the dream will probably be fairly obvious. The nature of the abandonment may be practical, or emotional. The feeling may have been projected by someone in your family who is feeling abandoned, and you are picking this up in your dream. Perhaps someone who is feeling betrayed needs your help or your friendship; don't let them down! It sometimes happens that the dream is reflecting your own feelings of guilt about something that happened in the past, and over which you had no real control. If there is a way to make amends, it might be as well to do so.

See also: LABYRINTH; LOST

ABBEY *An ancient church, large and impressive*

If it is a functioning abbey where services are held

Your own emotions are being reflected by this magnificent building, the timeless seat of grand state occasions, reinforcing a feeling of need for authority and stability. We all need something or somebody to rely on. This dream symbol is expressive of the need for a firm foundation on which to stand, but not in a way that makes any demand on yourself personally.

If the abbey is a picturesque ruin

The dream symbol points out that ancient certainties have been destroyed or allowed to decay to make way for modern ideas – and it probably relates to some recent event that has affected you deeply. Your own mood during the dream will do much to explain its nature: a pious or submissive feeling suggests that you are looking for something that once had reality, something very valuable and beautiful. This 'something' is your own early childhood, for a new-born baby is still attached to the higher world of spirit. The symbol of a ruined abbey may also represent a parent-figure on whom you used to rely. You may be feeling nostalgic for all the comfort and reassurances you once received but which are no longer available except as fond memories.

If it is a ruined abbey, bleak and ghost-haunted

Great abbeys used to be the centres of power in the land, where tithe barns and the abbot's tax gatherers may have spread fear or resentment among the local population. If your feelings during the dream were unpleasant, some recent event may have reminded you of an unpleasant type of authority that you were glad to get rid of. Take special heed if your child tells you about this type of dream. Some people have unpleasant memories of their schooldays, and the dream could recall those times, particularly if something or someone seems to be trying to establish a similarly unpleasant authority over the dreamer.

If it is a romantic ivy-clad Gothic ruin

In warm sunlight, or perhaps by moonlight, a building of this type is a perfect place for romance. Your feelings during the dream will give you a clue, especially if you had companions in the dream: are these people known to you or unknown? Are they real people, or purely imaginary? This could be no more than a wish fulfilment dream in which the beautiful abbey is seen as a beauty spot suitable for a romantic liaison.

See also: ALTAR; CATHEDRAL; CHURCH; RUINS

ABUSE   *Casting blame and insults*

If someone is hurling abuse at you

There may be a hidden element of self-criticism involved in this dream. Have you deserved censure in some way? It may be that the person in the dream is complaining about something which you know does not deserve blame: in this case your dream is being kind to your feelings by disguising the real complaint. You may have been feeling guilty, at a deep level, and blaming yourself about something that is not featured in your dream – something for which you were indeed to blame. Try using free association to find out what it really is: this could be your own subconscious way of concealing your true guilt, by acting out a dream charade.

If you are hurling abuse at someone else

This probably does not relate to any actual incident, but if the person is known to you in real life, you may have hurt their feelings in some way, perhaps inadvertently, and these are the feelings you are picking up in the dream. Dreams are seldom interested in blaming other people or complaining about them treating you unfairly; their chief purpose is to observe and correct your own actions and reactions. Hurting people's feelings can do more harm than one might suppose; the hurt penetrates to a very deep level and reflects back on you. A dream of this type is pointing out that you may be the culprit in this respect!

See also: ACCUSATIONS, ANGER

ABYSS *A great gaping hole in the ground*

If you have just discovered an abyss

The dream is bringing you to the awareness of your own unconscious mind. You may find yourself remembering things that happened to you many years ago and which you had completely forgotten; or, equally, you may be in danger of ignoring or neglecting responsibilities that other people have thrust upon you. Remember the unpleasant as well as the pleasant things that happen, and learn from them rather than trying to shut them out.

If you are looking down into a dream abyss

Take note of your feelings, your mood, during this dream episode. Whatever your feelings about the abyss, they reflect your habitual attitude towards your own most deeply hidden characteristics. Trigger events may have occurred recently which reminded you subconsciously of old patterns of behaviour, long forgotten. Their influence is still active deep inside you!

If you are almost falling into the abyss

This dream may be warning you to tread more carefully in some real life situation. Perhaps your present course of action or pattern of behaviour is threatening to end in disaster. A hole into which you seem in danger of falling can symbolise problems with relationships: you may be in danger of losing your job, or of going 'over the edge' in some very real way. Take careful stock of your current situation in life. If there seem to be no real-life people in the dream, it could be that you have become too dependent upon rules and moral principles. Some situations in life need a sentimental approach, with sympathetic understanding.

If you are actually falling into the dream abyss

The dream is telling you that you are being swamped by the contents of your own unconscious mind. You may have been feeling guilty over things that happened – perhaps long ago, perhaps recently – but it is up to you now to put matters right. Take careful note of any people known to you who appeared in the dream, because they will be closely involved in these matters.

If you are throwing rubbish into the abyss

This dream means that you have been neglecting to deal with matters that need your personal attention. You have probably been pushing unpleasant thoughts or onerous duties away, or perhaps you have been putting blame on someone else when it would make you much happier and better balanced if you faced up to these matters and dealt with them yourself.

If something or someone is pushing you into the abyss

It is important to identify the people or things or animals featuring in the dream, because in waking life they are probably being wrongly treated by you: they are asking you to search your conscience; you may have been ignoring their needs when you could well be dealing them and their problems more positively.

If you are pushing a person or an animal into the abyss

The implication is that you are ignoring or hurting these people or animals in real life. It may even be an archetype of the unconscious mind which you do not wish to face. You are trying to push these things out of your mind, but they and the problems they represent will not just disappear; they need to be dealt with by you firmly but kindly in real life. If not, unpleasant memories and guilt-feelings will return to haunt you when you are least expecting it.

If you are actually inside the abyss and searching around

Especially if there are other creatures down there, the dream implies that you are 'soul-searching' – exploring your own deeply hidden contents – which is probably showing itself in real life as depression. Your conscious mind may suffer a set-back, but in the long run the experience should be of great value to you.

If there are monsters or demons stirring in the abyss

We all have faults, peculiarities and feelings of guilt, though these may have been hidden since childhood. Some trigger event will have happened to bring these forgotten characteristics back to your awareness. Dream monsters like this are usually connected with sex impulses. Thinking quietly about them may make their true identity clear, and then you will be able to do something positive to clear out those old demons.

See also: CAVE; CELLAR; DUNGEON; PIT

ACCIDENT *An unexpected disruption to your normal progress*

If you dream of an accident while going about your everyday business

If in the dream you are on the move, by foot or bicycle or public transport, this has the nature of a warning dream. An accident or near-accident implies that you are in danger of suffering some sort of material loss, or of running up against financial or legal problems. Analyse the dream and if necessary use your association of ideas to help you think round the possibilities. Take careful note of your feelings – or the theme mood – during the dream; your emotions may contain a hint about the severity of the dream accident should it prove to have a counterpart in waking life. To be forewarned is to be forearmed.

If you have an accident while driving

Most dreams of accidents involve driving, especially if a car is your usual mode of transport – and even more so if it is your usual way of getting to work each morning. Cars, mechanical travel in general, or even simple metal objects, are all symbols of materiality, and in dreams they usually represent your own normal progress through life. When you dream there is an accident, or a near miss, or if there seems to be a strong risk of a possible accident, the implication is that either you or those who depend upon you are at risk of facing material loss. This is certainly a warning dream, though its implications may be purely abstract. If you have been pursuing a risky course in real life, use the dream to good advantage by taking heed of the warning. A railway crossing or road junction is often the scene of a dream accident, and this implies that someone else, possibly someone in competition with you, will be closely involved. A car crash or near miss involving a train at a crossing implies that your 'private' vehicle has run up against opposition from a 'public' vehicle. In this case you may assume that legal difficulties are a distinct possibility.

If you dream that someone else has damaged your car

This kind of accident, caused by others but involving your own means of travel through life, implies that people who rely on you in some way are entangling you in their private problems. You may have let your property or goods out to some other person, and the implications then will be fairly obvious. Or if someone related to you, a son or daughter perhaps, is involved in some enterprise that you have struggled to build up, there is a grave danger that they will cause harm to your affairs through their negligence.

See also: CAR; DRIVING; ROAD

ACCUSATIONS   *Ascribing blame*

If you dream that you are accusing someone

Some deep-seated personal fears or worries on your part are being aired in this dream, and perhaps you have been looking for someone to blame. If the person on the receiving end is a real person known to you, the dream is pointing out that you have probably been treating them unfairly in some way. Dreams are rarely concerned with blaming someone else: take it as a hint to 'consider the beam in thine own eye' – it may turn out to be yourself who deserves the criticism!

If you dream that someone is accusing you

There is likely to be a strong element of personal guilt hidden inside a dream in which someone is making an allegation about you. If the dream is of a real life situation involving real life people, of course you will recognize the fact. If not, it could be your own guilty conscience at work. The real cause for an accusation will probably be encrypted in the dream, and will need unscrambling through your own *Association of ideas.*

See also: ABUSE

ACNE   *Your complexion has become unsightly*

If dream pimples mark your face

Young people normally suffer from acne, and that cannot be helped. But your complexion or the condition of your skin often symbolise your habitual way of expressing your persona – the image of yourself that you want others to see and accept. In a dream, acne on your face means that your faults are on the surface, and obvious to others.

If dream acne affects a part of the body normally kept covered up

The implication is that you are keeping some unsavoury truth about yourself a secret from others (a common enough situation in real life) and feeling worried lest it be discovered.

See also: CLOTHES; NAKED

ACROBATICS   *Possessing amazing agility*

When you dream that someone else is the acrobat

We might say that someone is 'bending over backwards' to do something, meaning that they are going to great lengths, usually to do someone a favour or accommodate their needs. We might say that someone could do something or other 'standing on their head', meaning that they find the task easy. When someone you know seems in the dream to have become an acrobat, they may have been doing you a favour in real life. But more likely it will mean that you or they have made the best of a situation and performed a symbolic somersault to find a more secure foothold in life – a better job, perhaps, or a more rewarding position in society.

When you dream that you are performing athletic feats

Your own inner feelings are showing you that the inner self is not bound by the usual laws of materiality or gravity, being unencumbered by the physical body. Note any other features of the dream carefully, for dreams of this nature usually carry a powerful and very personal message.

See also: AGILITY

ACTORS   *Putting on a performance*

If you are the one doing the acting

The implication of this dream is that you have not been altogether honest in your real life relationships. Of course there are many reasons which compel us to modify our behaviour which are not necessarily dishonest; but this dream is suggesting that you are not altogether happy with this particular deception.

If others are doing the acting

The same principle applies: either you have seen through someone else's little deception, or the dream may be warning you to beware of insincerity on someone's part. If you know the dream actors in your personal life, the meaning of the dream will probably be fairly obvious to you; but a dream involving anonymous actors performing may be implying that someone with whom you are associated will prove unreliable.

If the actors you see in the dream are real, recognisable actors

They may be characters perhaps from a favourite TV show, or a film if this has a definite meaning for you. In this case the presence of real actors in your dream underlines the feelings you have for them. If, for instance, you feel that a certain TV soap is typical of normal, everyday life, and if your dream features characters from that series, they will be setting the dream-scene for you as a normal, everyday situation. But if they are from a show or a film that you thought spiteful or unpleasant in some way, then that kind of behaviour will be the context of your dream. Always remember your own feelings with regard to these dream figures: they will provide the clue.

See also: THEATRE

ADVERSARY *A mysterious, threatening character*

This dream character is likely to be one of the archetypes of the unconscious mind, but it can sometimes be identified as the personal shadow itself. The adversary represents any major factor that you have not been facing up to in waking life, and by ignoring it you have allowed it to build itself up in your subconscious mind until it has assumed menacing proportions. Any specific worry or temporary difficulty that has not been dealt with by your conscious mind may appear in dreams as an assailant rather than an adversary, which has a more permanent nature. Try to face up to the image and identify it: the dream itself should provide the clue. Though menacing, it cannot really harm you, as it is probably already a part of your own psyche. However, an aggressive or threatening figure in your dream, whether a person or an animal, may carry some kind of identifying feature that will enable you to place it in terms of your work, your relationships, or your family life. If you can put a name to this cryptic fear, you will be better able to deal with it.

See also: ASSAILANT; DEMON; OPPONENT; XENOPHOBIA

ADVICE *Handing over helpful information*

If you dream you are being given advice by someone you know

If the adviser is a reliable sort of person known to you personally, you will probably be able to relate the dream incident to an incident in waking life, and understand what the dream is trying to tell you. It will certainly be a personal matter that only you can interpret successfully.

If you are being advised by an unknown wise person

Though this friendly figure is not known to you in real life, it may

114

in fact be a part of your own self – an archetype of the unconscious mind. In this case you would do well to heed their advice. because it will certainly be of great value to you. It is your own best advice to yourself!

If you dream you are giving advice to someone else

The dream could be warning you not to interfere where you are not wanted. Note who you are giving the advice too, and how does that person react? Your dream advice, of course, is not necessarily *bad* advice, but never jump to conclusions; think it over and look at these various possibilities objectively and thoroughly.

See also: GODDESS; KING; QUEEN; WISE PERSON

AGILITY   *Unusual physical abilities*

If you are performing amazing contortions in your dream

The inner feelings are not bound by physical laws, or even the *thought* of physical laws. In dreams, unencumbered by your sleeping body, you can defy the force of gravity! This can be very encouraging, but it can have a negative side: the dream may be pointing out that you have been evading your responsibilities or are hiding some truth which would be better released. By dancing in the air you may be hurting someone's feelings in real life, and this can do more harm than you might at first think.

If you dream someone known to you is performing physical feats

Perhaps you have been trying to pin this person down in some way, and are finding it very difficult. They seem to have an unfair advantage which you envy, perhaps. This is a reflection of your own feelings rather than the feelings of this other person who probably does not want to become involved.

See also: ACROBATICS

ALTAR   *A sacred place*

If you are merely observing an altar in your dream

Whether you are a religious person or not, an altar represents the centre of worship and devotion within your feelings – the place that you would not want to see defiled with anything you normally dissociate from that feeling of special importance. Different people have differing principles, and will be devoted to different things, but at the heart of everyone's feelings, symbolically, is the table of the altar, the holy of holies. It may be associated with the feelings you have for another person. Perhaps you feel that your relationship is not openly acceptable for some reason, and you would like to make it so.

If you are placing something on the altar in your dream

If you can identify the object you have placed there, it is sure to have great significance for you, and only you can interpret the dream fully. If you are not sure what the object was, think round it very carefully, using your association of ideas. Remember too if anything else was already on the altar, for this may offer a clue. The symbol of an altar may represent either a principle which you already consider to be beyond reproach, or a circumstance that you would dearly like to make acceptable and free from feelings of guilt.

See also: ABBEY; CATHEDRAL; CHURCH

ANGEL   *A supernatural being*

The concept of the world dream explains how the angel-principle should be regarded in relation to our everyday world. As dream symbols, angels serve to balance the world of nature, their presence acting as a counterbalance to both Freudian dreams and Adlerian dreams. Within the human psyche angels comprise the antithesis of the aggressive 'plant-nature' and the competitive, often sex-obsessed 'animal nature' in ourselves. Precisely what an angel means for you will depend almost entirely on your own experiences in life, your own ideas of what if anything constitutes 'an angel' and what you suppose the function of an angel to be. In most cultures they are thought of as divine messengers, and made of light. When their dream image is drawn from the collective unconscious they are able to represent whatever the will of God is perceived to be by the individual, in any given set of circumstances.

If you dream of an angel, and this is a good experience

Do angels really exist or are they merely symbols of a higher life form about which we know nothing? In the West, it is usual to think of angels as gentle beings who might be relied upon to give a helping hand when it is most needed: loving, forgiving, sexless and impartial. If your dream angel appeared to you in what you think of as its typical typical western form, winged, robed and filled with love, the message it conveys will be one of reassurance, condolence and possibly gentle reproof.

If meeting your dream angel was an unpleasant experience

In some countries, especially in the East, angels are thought of in an unsentimental way as divine administrators, doling out judgment, punishment or reward as it may be deserved. They may be seen as fierce masculine beings wielding a sword or battleaxe. If your dream angel was like this, you can be sure that it was bearing a message: one that you do not want to listen to in waking life. Try to fathom out what this message is, because it is certain to be an important matter of conscience. If an angel appears before you in a dawn dream, you should be in no doubt about the message: it will be for you alone.

    See also: JUDGE

ANGER

If you are the angry one in the dream

Dream anger is often expressed when someone during the day has drawn attention to a personal characteristic that you are sensitive about and may be acting as a barrier to your peace of mind. They may have done this quite unconsciously, provoking a defensive response by hinting at this flaw in your character. The idea of 'righteous indignation' sounds reasonable when the other person seems to be in the wrong; but justifiable anger seldom happens in the dream world. Dream anger usually suggests that something is psychologically wrong – something that ought to be put right.

If someone else is the angry one

Anger can sometimes actually be seen in a dream, like a dark cloud issuing from the angry character's mouth; sometimes it can be smelled as a rotten-plant smell. A dream of this nature may be purely informative if your own well-being has been compromised. But sometimes the emotion becomes transferred during a dream, so that the person who triggered your own anger appears to be the angry one instead. In either case, dream anger is likely to imply that your inner feelings know that a change of attitude is needed on your part, but your thoughts and everyday emotions are unwilling to face up to this in waking life. Dreams featuring anger call for personal interpretation by thinking round each incident in the dream sequence and trying to identify any mental or emotional barriers. They are sure to exist, and you would be better off without them.

See also: ABUSE; ACCUSATIONS

ANIMALS *Any living non-human creatures*

If you seem to have become an animal in your dream

A dream like this may be an interesting reflection of the world dream, or it may even be a reincarnation dream. Very often, though, the dreamer may have been wondering or imagining what it would be like to be an animal of this sort, and the dream is granting your wish to find out.

If animals feature in your dream

Somebody like a farmer or perhaps a zoo-keeper, to whom animals are particularly familiar, is likely to find them included as a background feature in a dream, merely to set the scene in familiar surroundings. But where this is obviously not the case, a personal interpretation will be needed. Heavy, horned animals, usually bulls, carry with them the idea of powerful masculinity best not disturbed. As a simple warning, or perhaps to reflect an anxiety already present in the dreamer's mind, their appearance may suggest that the dreamer should take care not to upset the kind of man who may fit this category in real life. A shy forest animal such as a startled deer among the trees may be telling you that you have been evading your social obligations, taking refuge instead in the 'forest of the mind'. If a person close to you in waking life, has been behaving like a particular type of animal – perhaps greedy like a pig, or cruel and fierce like a wolf, or liable to charge blindly like a bull, or rampage like a rhinoceros – they may well assume this animal guise in your dream.

If you dream of your pet animals

The dream may be offering a practical message about your pets, and some people have gleaned useful information in this way. But sometimes the personal shadow can take the form of a fierce animal, and when it does so this dream animal is often a travesty or distortion of a domestic pet familiar to the dreamer. Sometimes it becomes a terrifying nightmare, but it is a fairly common dream occurrence which draws attention to the fact that this apparently demonic creature represents something that is actually very close and familiar – a part of the dreamer's own psyche which has built itself up into this frightening form within the unconscious mind. It could be a stern warning if you or a family member has been dabbling in the occult..

See also: BIRDS; BULL; COCKEREL; DEMON; DOG; COW; EAGLE; ELEPHANT; HORSE; PARROT; PIG; WOLF; ZOO

ANTIQUE   *Something very old and valuable*

The collective unconscious includes contents that probably date back many thousands of years to the dawn of human awareness, and this vast psychological sea is the most likely source of an antique that features in your dream. This is all the more probable if the dream is a particularly vivid one – and even more so if it comes to you as a dawn dream.

If someone known to you shows or gives you an antique in your dream

You can be certain that this person is offering you something of great spiritual benefit. They want to share with you a secret, a desire, or a practical quality that you would be unwise to reject. Purely on a psychological basis – that is, without a potentially spiritual content – the antique could represent sexual impulses or a hoped-for sexual relationship. In mystical terms, while the sexual element is not precluded, the dream may be pointing to a spiritual path now open to you.

If no-one else is involved in this dream of an antique

The dream object represents something, or some abstract quality, that is very precious to you: something rooted in the past that affects you strongly, and which you do not feel able to express in more realistic terms. The dream object may be a chest, or a casket, or a cupboard, or some other container, and in this case you can be sure that it contains something of great value or lasting significance. In mythology, Pandora's box contained all the passions and problems of the world, which escaped when it was opened, leaving only hope in the box. This is usually seen as a symbol of marriage with all its ups and downs, blessings and frustrations. The dream antique is very much a personal symbol, and only the dreamer will be able to think round all the implications and possibilities connected with it, and reach a satisfactory conclusion.

See also: ARCHEOLOGY; VASE

ARCHEOLOGY   *Digging up secrets from the past*

If ancient artefacts are being dug from the ground

Anything in your dream that is being revealed from its ancient hiding place, or anything that seems on the point of being revealed, is likely to represent some piece of information or new understanding coming to conscious awareness. In effect, you have been digging into the depths of your own personal unconscious. The implication of this dream is that this knowledge has been hidden for a very long time; it may even represent something inherited from your ancestors – a family secret which should now be revealed to you. Whatever it is, it is likely to have psychological significance, though it may have no material value. Only you, the dreamer, can discover the true meaning.

If an ancient corpse or skeleton is being exhumed

This could be the symbol of some factor, some idea, some principle, long gone and forgotten, that is now being revived. You may well feel that it should be allowed to remain forgotten. But it can also signify the 'bones' of a new idea based on ancient understanding – an idea that may have useful potential.

See also: ANTIQUE; BONES; PIT; SKELETON

ART *The creation of pleasing images*

If you are an artist in your dream

It may be that you are in fact an artist, and creating artwork is typical of your everyday life, in which case the dream-sequence is merely setting the scene for the rest of the dream as an everyday affair. But if art does not normally play a part in your life, the dream plainly shows that some sort of creative work is being done or planned: something is being prepared perhaps for public viewing. The inspiration for your artwork is likely to arise from your own personality, and represents an aspect of yourself that you feel shows you in a good light. It could also mean that you are trying to show some object or situation in a better light by falsifying the details, or presenting a somewhat exaggerated view.

If you are watching an artist at work in your dream

Unless the artist is a person known to you in real life, he or she could be one of the archetypes of the unconscious mind , making a point for your information. It may be the persona, painting a sweetened view of your best profile. The dream suggests that you are falsifying your position in some way not altogether pleasing to your conscience. If the painter is a real acquaintance or family member, the likelihood is that they are the one presenting the 'prettied-up' view, and trying to pull the wool over your eyes.

See also: PAINTING

ASSAILANT *An unknown dream-enemy or opponent*

One of the archetypes of the unconscious mind, the assailant is a dream figure representing matters which the dreamer has found upsetting or challenging, and has not been able to deal with during waking hours. Perhaps you have been hoping that some problem will go away by ignoring it, but problematic things do not go away permanently: they are pushed into your unconscious mind, to be dealt with by the inner feelings. If there is still no satisfactory conclusion they are liable to become absorbed by the personal shadow. A dream assailant is broadly similar to the archetype of the adversary, but tends to represent a one-off circumstance, something from outside oneself. A dream adversary relates to a permanent predicament – a long-term condition existing within the psyche. The actual nature of your assailant will probably be obscure in the dream, and it may simply be felt as an unseen, threatening presence. Analyse the dream carefully by thinking round every detail, noting your emotions at every stage, and listing any associated ideas and themes – especially if you find them vaguely upsetting: these may hold the clue!

See also: ADVERSARY; OPPONENT

AUTUMN *Past the prime*

This is quite a common dream metaphor: the fall of the year marks the end of warm sunshine, flowers and greenery. Plant life at least is drawing to a close, or approaching its season of dormancy in a brief spectacle of colour. A poetic comparison with the 'autumn of our years' has always been compelling, and when autumn features in your dream this is its probable significance. Perhaps you are feeling no longer young, and looking forward – with eagerness, or resignation, or perhaps trepidation – to your own declining years. But the symbol may not be referring to the dreamer's age: to dream you are walking through a forest with falling leaves usually suggests that an easy phase of your life has passed its climax and is approaching full cycle. It may not be a bad thing. Look on it as the 'season of mellow fruitfulness', a quiet period when you can take stock for the future. The approaching winter may be no more than a resting period until the time for spring regrowth.

See also: CLOCK; FOREST

BABY   *A very young child*

The innocent child self is a major archetype of the unconscious mind and expresses the essence of the individual, the basic self without all its habits and hang-ups, without having been influenced by the world around it, without what some would call 'character' or 'personality'. A blank sheet, in effect, upon which all the varying impressions of the world are recorded as life goes on.

If you dream of a very young or new-born baby

This is most likely to symbolise any new creation or new idea that has come to light – a new enterprise, a new career, a new understanding, or a new way of looking at a familiar situation. A baby is innocent, naive, 'silly' in the original sense of the word. The dream may be pointing out your own reactions to some completely unfamiliar set of circumstances. Suppose you move to a strange country, or join a group of people with unfamiliar ideas, you may feel a bit 'silly', and the dream will be reflecting your own inner feelings. But, as always, there may be a more straightforward and obvious meaning to the dream symbol – you may have been thinking a lot about babies for whatever reason – or it may be referring to an actual baby in your family, and the dream should then be interpreted in personal terms.

See also: CHILD

BALL   *A solid sphere*

You may of course be a wizard at some ball game, and your dreams may well reflect this – only you can know. But a ball can be a highly significant dream symbol. Psychic wholeness can be symbolised by a sphere or a ball, and if you are consciously working towards this psychological and spiritual goal, the 'self' may well be featured as a ball that is aimed at the goal.

If you dream that you see a ball bouncing or rolling

124

This symbol can imply that you are finding yourself at odds with the rest of society, or with your own community. Ball games such as football and baseball are hugely popular, of course, and it often seems that the crowd in a stadium are totally at unison, totally orientated towards some 'goal', all acting as one. Opposing sides and their supporters will be a mirror image of the other side, and their orientation is equally single-minded. This could be what your dream is telling you. The ball is the neutral odd one out in the game, and this could apply to you, in the game of life.

If you dream that you are bouncing the ball yourself

This reflects the feeling that you are in complete harmony with your own particular surroundings and the people around you: you are at ease with yourself and with your relationships. However, the dream may be implying that you have been ignoring the needs of some minority group, or that you have become too partisan in your commitments. It could be an important symbol warning you to take stock of your attitude to others.

    See also: BALLOON

BALLET   *Graceful physical conformity*

If you have only recently started taking an interest in your dreams, when you dream of ballet dancers you will probably merely be watching them perform. If your dream studies are fairly well advanced, however, you will very likely be taking part in the dance yourself. In either case it will have a personal significance. In effect, ballet is the art of telling a story set to music, by way of graceful physical movements. Poise and confidence both play a large part, and ballet training must involve a great deal of strain and suffering before the dancers get it right. It can perhaps become obsessive, for the true feelings of the performers have to remain subdued or hidden: everyone has to follow the correct routine. If you know the dream dancers in real life – not necessarily as real dancers but as your everyday friends and colleagues – the dream may be demonstrating your admiration for their expertise in whatever they normally do. The dream is expressing your own deep emotions, and your mood during the dream or shortly after waking may be important as a pointer. Ballet dancers, in effect, are wearing a disguise, and this may suggest that deception of some sort is taking place. The dream may be expressing your own sorrow or sense of resignation or guilt at being forced to 'play a part' in life, never free to follow your conscience or your own preferences.

See also: ACTING; DANCE; THEATRE

BALLOON   *A free-floating sphere*

If you dream of a mysterious balloon

A bubble-like sphere floating over the earth is a fair description of the nature of your own inner feelings. Unaffected by the force of gravity, and unrestricted even by your physical body, the inner feelings are able to float free: the non-material side of your nature can rise above earthly cares and problems. This dream could be an invitation to look for a more spiritual path through life – and to practice recording and understanding your dreams is an excellent way to start.

If you dream of a child's balloon

The symbol will be reflecting the carefree feelings of innocence normally associated with party balloons. Balloons of this sort suggest material enjoyment, either innocent or not-so-innocent, and may be indicating a real situation of which you are well aware. If other people who are known to you in real life appear in the dream, their pleasure-seeking ways may be heading for a setback. But if no other recognisable person features in your dream, it could be a gentle warning that all good things must come to an end: your balloon may burst at any time. Whatever situation you are currently putting your trust in does not seem to have a reliable future.

If you dream of a hot-air balloon

A passenger-carrying balloon can have a similar meaning to either of the above alternatives: the context of the dream should make the symbol clear. The implication is that the passengers are being raised above the common run of humanity; they are being lifted by heat – and the dream-source of heat is usually the passions – the intensity of people's outward feelings. But man-made balloons have to land sooner or later, and passions are liable to change. There is an element of desire or wishful thinking about this dream – the wish that you could really float above the world and its problems.

See also: BALL; FLYING

BAMBOO   *Symbol of flexibility*

Like the willow, as a universally understood symbol, bamboo expresses the propensity to yield to a more powerful force, to bend before the hurricane. The stoutest tree may be uprooted or broken off in a gale, but the bamboo, whilst green and growing, though bent double, will spring up again unharmed. The application to circumstances in waking life is likely to be obvious: it is better to yield to whatever powerful force cannot be controlled or resisted, rather than risk destruction. As a warning dream, the image of bamboo bending in the wind could be telling you not to fight against unreasonable odds, whatever the real-life situation may be: find a way to let the troubles pass safely over your head. If the real-life situation is not clear to you, try to remember if anyone or anything else featured in your dream, for they may provide the clue. You, yourself, are probably the 'bamboo', but you may still need to identify the 'gale'. Or perhaps you, or some aspect of your personality, which is represented by the hurricane, in which case it is the bamboo that will need identifying. Without malicious intent, you could be hurting someone else's feelings quite unwittingly.

See also: AGILITY; BULLYING; HURRICANE

BARN   *A storage building*

There is always the possibility that your dream is of a *real* barn in a real situation, with a personal meaning for you. But more frequently a dream barn symbolises the self, and in particular, perhaps, that part of the self that you are not normally aware of – the personal unconscious mind and its contents. This image is being presented by your own inner feelings, probably in the light of recent real-life occurrences, so it is likely to carry a strong personal message.

If you dream that the barn is empty

Emptiness is the feeling that the dream is portraying: you may have been feeling that your life is empty, or meaningless, or worthless. Your barn should be full of contents, even if they are only your hopes and fears, and if you dream of the barn again, it may well seem to have become miraculously filled with valuable possessions. The inner feelings often present an illusion – a white lie dream, perhaps – intended to set your mind on a different and more positive track.

If you dream that someone is in the barn

This dream character may seem harmless, or perhaps mysterious and threatening. Unless of course it is a real person known to you in waking life, this mysterious figure is an image arisen from the unconscious mind. A dream such as this implies that you have been pushing some problem aside rather than facing up to it in waking life. It may be a long-term problem, perhaps a repressed memory or psychological block that is affecting your peace of mind. Or it may be a short-term challenge, some problem that has arisen recently and which is worrying you. It may even be your own shadow, composed of some of your own characteristics which you want no-one – not even yourself – to know about. Remember that it is your own dream barn, symbolising your personal unconscious mind, so take some trouble to think round each dream feature very carefully, and arrive at an honest interpretation.

See also: ADVERSARY; ASSAILANT; HUT; STORE; VASE

BATTLE   *Group aggression*

Occasionally, personal aggression or taking part in a battle is a feature of a balancing dream that is compensating for an unusually gentle lifestyle, and equally you may dream of attacking people as a way of compensating for an overly defensive attitude in daily life. But as a rule attacking someone or defending yourself in a dream tends symbolically to reflect your current situation in everyday life. You may have been feeling that everyone is against you: it is a common experience to feel that you are the odd one out, or under siege, and fearing that your position is being undermined by the actions of others. People can become paranoid if they feel they are being persecuted – and of course such a feeling may well turn out to be justified. Life often seems like a battlefield too when you are simply trying to improve your lot in the material sphere. In general, dreams of aggression call for an appraisal of your own lifestyle: your dream battle may be warning you against selfish or hurtful behaviour. Remember that the cycle of tit-for-tat is only likely to be broken by modifying your own attitude – bearing in mind not only the immediate benefit, but long-term relationships too.

See also: ANGER

BATTLEMENTS   *Security against assault*

Security is the key-word where this dream symbol is concerned, but security for a definite reason – either you or someone else in the dream is under threat. This may be your situation in waking life: you feel the need to defend yourself, and this may seem well justified. But the assault is liable to increase while you cower behind your dream battlements. Similarly if some other person is finding safety against your own attacks: there will be a genuine reason for the dream, and you should come to a conclusion about the wisdom of pursuing your current course in life.

See also: BATTLE; FORTRESS; TOWER

BIRDS

In all times and places where superstition has played a large part in daily life, birds have habitually been thought of as omens, and some traces of this can be recognised even in civilised lands today: magpies may be thought to predict several different kinds of fate dependent on the number that gather together; owls are said to be harbingers of death, and ravens too are supposed to foretell death, danger or disaster; storks are supposed to bring good luck, and newborn babies. The 'ominous' connection with birds relates to the fact that, being free to fly around, they are liable to appear almost anywhere at any time, and this makes them ideal as harbingers of whatever we may have in mind. To people everywhere, no matter how sophisticated they may seem, particular birds tend to call to mind specific associations, some based on ancient tradition, as the white dove of peace and relief from trouble. Wild geese irresistibly bring to mind far away wild and marshy places; the 'blue bird' has come to signify happiness if it flies around a house or perches on the roof; the parrot is in a class of its own, as are the eagle and the cockerel. If you have definite ideas about birds of different kinds, if they remind you of some or other human function, or if they always seem to behave in a certain way, in your dream they may represent that function or type of behaviour for you. Different nationalities have different bird symbols of this nature. Birds, it seems to us, can range from fierce and rapacious (think of vultures – or perhaps great flocks of seed-eating birds that sometimes devastate a peasant farmer's crops), to gentle and lovable; their voices range from the delightful songs of one to the harsh croak or screech of another. A large white bird flying away is a universally held symbol of the human soul leaving the body. Dead birds almost equally universally signify lost freedom, lost hopes – a situation such as marriage which has become routine and restrictive. In ancient times omens often involved birds; today, most live birds as dream symbols, like omens, can mean whatever the individual unconsciously assumes them to mean.

See also: ANIMALS

BLOOD   *Essence and energy*

The vitality and driving passions of life may be symbolised by blood, and in some systems of religious thought or spiritual understanding a person is considered to possess different 'bloods' representing different basic passions: these symbolic bloods are not all red – red is merely the colour of the energetic, aggressive and defensive passion. The passion of learning and observing, or its blood, is thought to be white; the life-blood of sexual passion is considered to be yellow; the life-blood of greed and material possession is said to be black. If dream-blood seems to have changed colour, its message may follow these lines. Typically, though, dream-blood is the real physical blood that keeps us alive. A person bleeding or wearing blood-stained clothing in a dream usually signifies the onset of illness connected with the heart. Clothes of a faded or dull red can imply that the wearer or onlooker in the dream has been worrying about their health, but the potential illness is not presenting an immediate danger.

See also: DOCTOR

BOAT   *The means of riding over water*

Water as a dream symbol represents the feelings – emotions and sexual impulses. A boat symbolises a person's passage over these sometimes troubled waters.

If you dream your boat is floating smoothly over deep water

The very fact that you have dreamed about it implies that you are feeling some apprehension; it suggests that you are well aware of the depth of emotion or passion beneath you, and feel the need for caution.

If you dream of a large ocean liner

In days gone by, these large ships became established as the obvious symbol of overseas travel, and so, by implication, an indication of a complete change of life scene, a thorough uprooting of everything familiar. Now of course, their place has been taken by jet airliners, and large sea-going ships are typical of leisurely holidays – and thence of a welcome change of scene, but not a permanent change.

If you dream of sailing over stormy waters

This suggests that you are currently passing through a very stormy phase in your emotional relationships. You seem to have become very deeply embroiled in some scene which you may find difficult to back out of. Your feelings are being 'tossed around'.

If your boat capsizes in the dream

The implication is that some emotional or sexual situation in which you are involved is proving 'all too much', and you are being swamped by your own feelings, your own turbulent passions.The symbol will probably prove to have a very personal meaning.

See also: WATER

BOG   *A very sticky patch*

If you dream that you can see a bog ahead

(Or a quagmire, a slough, a morass, a marsh, or a mire – the dream symbol may be given a variety of names), take it as a warning that there may be sticky times ahead. A situation exists in real life which must be avoided for your own safety or security. The dream symbol calls for a change at least of emphasis, if not of direction, in your everyday life.

If you dream you are standing on quaking ground

Solid ground represents the solidity of materiality; on a personal scale it represents the security of your normal situation in life, your job, your marriage, your relationships, your living conditions. There may have been a trigger event recently to make you doubt the reliability of things you used to depend upon. This could be classified as a warning dream.

If you dream you are plunging ever deeper into mud

The implication could scarcely be clearer: you need to consider a change of direction regarding whatever you most closely associate with these muddy conditions. The symbol implies that your actions or behaviour have in some respects become unpleasant, even to yourself. If this is the case, a reappraisal of your lifestyle is overdue!

See also: MUD

BONES   *The basic framework*

As a dream symbol, bones can have several very different connotations: they can imply the 'bones of an idea' – something new that is being planned; or they can imply the discarded remains of something old and no longer of use. They can also represent the

133

strength within a scheme, the firm basis upon which an enterprise is founded. The theme mood or overriding emotion of your dream may help to explain the personal meaning of your dream symbol: if you recall the feeling of regret, or wistfulness, bones may represent the hopes and ideas you once had, but which came to nothing – something which you remember fondly and would perhaps like to resurrect. Dreams of bones can also involve a play on words – we speak of something being 'near the bone', meaning that it is rather hurtful, or we may 'have a bone to pick' with someone when we have a dispute. A bone featuring in your dream may also be a special sort of bone made known to you in the dream, and this will provide a clue.

See also: SKELETON

BOOKS   *Feeding the mind by reading*

Dream books almost always signify their own contents – the facts, the stories and ideas inside them – and a shelf full of books may represent a person who is full of ideas, a 'storehouse of knowledge'. In spiritual dreams you may perhaps dream of being given a book which will show you whatever answer you need, in words or pictures. In more mundane dreams a book will represent an important piece of knowledge you may be searching for, the information you urgently need. In a few cases, a background of books may symbolise a comfortable situation of some kind, or a privileged lifestyle carrying the implication of material wealth – but a background of knowledge and a wealth of ideas is the more usual interpretation. There are exceptions which will be entirely personal: books may, for instance, represent a certain person whom you associate with books for some reason. Quite commonly, if you pursue some particular subject or interest and like to read about it, a display of books in your dream may symbolise an extension of your opportunities in that direction.

See also: LIBRARY

BREAD   *The staff of life*

In countries where bread is not the usual staple, other food commodities such as root crops or rice or maize porridge may take its place as a dream symbol. Its meaning is likely to be 'the basic means of living', and of course the term 'bread' can also mean 'money'.

If you dream you are well stocked with bread

This reflects your own feelings about your current life situation. It may be a predictive dream telling of an imminent upturn in your fortunes – though it could equally well have the nature of a wish fulfilment dream, when it could prove to be no more than an expression of hope.

If you dream you have run out of bread

The implication is that your usual means of earning a living has disappeared, or is liable shortly so to do; your supply of 'bread' is drying up. This symbol is most likely to reflect your worries about security, or your own current fear that your position in life is not altogether reliable.

If you dream that your bread has gone stale, or mildewed

This dream reflects, or predicts, a disappointing situation; the remuneration or reward you had been expecting does not seem to be materialising. Perhaps someone on whom you have relied to supply an income or a regular service has let you down, or will shortly do so. In this case you need to start looking for a new source of 'bread'.

See also: FEAST; FOOD

BRIDGE   *The means to surmount an obstacle*

If you dream of a bridge over water

Water symbolises emotions and sexual desires, and a bridge across usually means that you are feeling anxious about some emotional encounter in your life. It implies that you do not really want to enter the water and get too wet: you do not want to become too involved. It may well refer to a sexual hang-up which you find troublesome, some issue that you would rather not face directly. The water in the dream may provide a clue. Dark or muddy water implies guilt and a sense of wrongdoing. Clear sparkling water shows that feelings of guilt are not involved, but the dream bridge implies that you would still rather avoid what you see as a tricky situation.

If you are looking down from a bridge

Take careful note of what you are looking down at; what you are crossing over. Whatever it is will probably be the crux of your dream. The dream bridge forms a very useful function, enabling you to take a clear look at whatever is bothering your waking mind, whatever you are anxious to avoid. You might be looking down on a busy main road, and the implication may be that you do not wish to follow the crowd. Perhaps you have been feeling superior to the popular view about some issue, or feel that you wish to be alone to pursue your own interests in peace. Or you might be looking down on a quiet country lane or a lonely track, and this could carry the opposite meaning: you have been feeling somewhat isolated and would prefer to join the crowd and play a more active part in mainstream society. A railway track running beneath the bridge can imply that you feel the need for a complete change of lifestyle: you need to get away from your current situation! If you are looking down at water running beneath the bridge, refer to the previous paragraph. The dream episode seems to imply that you have been feeling very emotional and rather apprehensive about the way your life is going.

If you dream you are passing beneath or looking up at a bridge

Bridges often feature in dreams when your waking life encounters difficulties. A fugitive, or someone who feels in some way an outcast of society will dream of a bridge which, if attained, can provide a means of overcoming social isolation and rejoining the world at a more rewarding level. A bridge overhead always reflects a feeling that there must be a better way forward, particularly if the ground beneath is unpleasant to walk or drive on, perhaps muddy or flooded with unpleasant emotions. Try to remember if the dream bridge featured anything that might offer further clues.

See also   FORD; ROAD; STEPPING STONES; WATER

BROOM   *A means of removing dirt*

Dirt, clutter, unwanted characteristics, unwanted people – a dream broom can represent a helping hand or a circumstance which seems about to remove any of these things. As the dreamer, you may be looking at the broom or the sweeper as though you yourself are part of the clutter to be swept away; or you may be the one doing the sweeping. The distinction will be obvious to you in the dream. The old saying 'a new broom sweeps clean' often applies when somebody like a new employer, or a newly appointed manager, wishes to reduce the workforce and is looking very keenly at standards of work and relationships. The dream can reflect the anxiety felt by those in line for redundancy.

See also: DIRT

BUGS   *Parasitic insects*

In America it is usual to call all insects 'bugs', but strictly this term should be reserved for those insects with sucking mouthparts. Whether these are plant-bugs or human bed-bugs, they are parasitic creatures in the sense that they suck the life-blood out of whatever it is they are feeding on. To dream that horrible insects are feeding on your own body, or are infesting your bed and personal belongings, seems to imply that you are aware that something – it may be an unwanted person or an unexpected circumstance – is taking advantage of you and using you in a way that you deeply resent. Similarly with a plant-bug; you may have a cherished plant, and find that these creatures are drawing out the sap which keeps the plant healthy. The plant in your dream may symbolise your own family, your business, or you yourself, and the implications are the same – you feel that some unwanted presence is taking advantage of you and sapping your resources. By itself, the dream offers no solution to the problem, but merely reflects your concern.

See also: ADVERSARY; ASSAILANT; INSECTS

BULL   *A powerful masculine animal*

In dreams a bull usually symbolises a man whom the dreamer is nervous of offending. In the normal way, such a 'bull-man' may be no trouble at all, but he could well prove dangerous if annoyed or challenged – not necessarily in a physical sense; it may well be a matter of business. If in your dream you find yourself tiptoeing or walking warily around a seemingly docile bull, this is likely to be the connotation: the symbol is reflecting your present concerns rather than warning of trouble ahead. A bull charging along and looking for trouble is a different matter – this could well be a warning dream implying that an angry male character – or anyone with powerful passions – is liable to cause you problems.

See also: ANIMALS

BULLYING   *Intimidating another person*

If you are the bully in your dream

138

The implication is that you have been acting in some unfair way, causing another person unnecessary anxiety or suffering. Perhaps it is only their feelings that are being hurt, but one's own inner feelings take this situation very seriously, as it causes unbalance in your own Self. Careful thought is needed to identify the problem. It may, however, be a balancing dream in which the dreamer is compensating for feelings of helplessness in real life.

If you are being bullied in your dream

It may simply mean that your peace of mind is often upset, and you disapprove of the way other people behave. But if you are actually suffering from bullying in real life the dream may be pointing out a possible course of action. Now is the time to decide to do something positive about it.

If you recognize the dream-bully as a real person known to you

There may be no real bullying by this person as far as you are aware, but it seems your own inner feelings are being disturbed by his actions, or by your own relationship with him or her. The dream offers you a chance to take a calmly objective look at the situation.

> *See also:*   ADVERSARY; ASSAILANT; OPPONENT

BULRUSHES   *Plant cover at the water's edge*

Water symbolises the feelings; pond or streamside vegetation symbolises a situation or an attitude of mind in which to hide from powerful feelings. From this hiding place, whatever is affecting you can be observed or felt, but you are hoping to remain uninvolved personally. Bulrushes or reeds in a dream usually seem to be hiding something – perhaps some wild creature representing your own sexual passions. Certainly something with a strongly emotional content is liable to emerge from it. Typically, rush-like plants feature in a dream when something highly significant seems about to emerge from a strongly emotional situation.

See also: WATER

BURGLAR   *An unwelcome intruder*

It is not unusual for a burglar to feature in a dream, and as a simple expression of anxiety the implications of intrusion or loss of privacy or possessions are fairly obvious.

If you dream that an unknown burglar is getting in

This may reflect your own worries about security, and the building where the burglary seems to be taking place may be your own home, or that of someone else closely connected with or reliant upon you. This is a straightforward, practical dream advising you to improve security. But it may also represent worries that your secrets are in danger of disclosure, and that you have been feeling guilty about something you would not like to become public knowledge.

If you dream that the burglar is known to you

The implication is that the person concerned seems to be interfering in your private affairs. It may be that bureaucracy or the law is involved in this. Any dream which features real characters known to you needs personal interpretation by thinking round all the details very carefully. The burglar breaking in may be yourself in disguise; you may be projecting your fears or feelings of guilt onto someone else; you may even be meddling in someone else's affairs – and only you can know the truth of the matter.

If you are prowling around in someone else's property

The chances are this dream reflects some recent situation know to you. Have you perhaps been trying to find out details about some organization, or perhaps a business acquaintance? The implication is that you are not too sure of your ground. You may not have feelings of guilt, but you do feel deep down that you are in the wrong. Perhaps the dream is hinting that you need to be more open about your intentions.

See also: ASSAILANT; ENEMY

BURIAL   *Disposing of the evidence*

If an official ceremony is involved

To dream of a burial is always unlikely to predict an actual death. The most likely implication seems to be that some important episode of your life is coming to a close, and that a new set of circumstances with new opportunities are about to arise. An important ceremony involving lots of people reflects the fact that the closing episode does indeed involve others. Take note of these people's reactions and attitudes, and your own feelings, as these will provide important pointers.

If the burial is a very simple affair

Unless there are other indications, the dream seems to be implying that you are pushing something out of sight – something that might be better made public. The grave could represent your own personal unconscious mind, in which you are trying to bury matters that should have been dealt with during waking hours.

See also: CORPSE; DEATH; FUNERAL; PIT

CACTUS   *Any thorny or prickly plant*

Cacti and other prickly succulent plants tend to grow in desert-like places with very dry conditions, and if you study the world dream

141

and Adlerian dreams you will see that plants growing in these conditions can carry a very powerful hint of the internal power struggle. You may be feeling rather like a cactus plant yourself, forced to survive in unrewarding circumstances and defending yourself against the assaults of others, real or imaginary. This dream may be telling you to have more confidence in yourself and in your friends and colleagues, and look for a practical way out from your problems. There is probably no need to be so defensive. But any thorny or prickly plants featuring in a dream symbolise dangers and difficulties which may be very real in your daily life. By itself the dream symbol is offering no solution, but simply reflecting your own feelings.

See also: DESERT; FOREST; SAND

CALENDAR   *A record or diary of days and dates*

There is always a hint of urgency in this symbol. It is reminding you of the passage of time for a reason. It can be a reminder that your time is limited and there are still many things to do. It may be reminding you of an important date or anniversary that you are in danger of overlooking. There are sure to be other factors in your dream which offer a clue. Calendars and diaries can refer backward as well as forward, and the symbol may be pointing out the significance of some past event that has suddenly become relevant in your life. It may be a reflection of the general feeling that 'time is running out', that a chance has arrived to lift your situation in life to a new level, perhaps with spiritual connotations. Two calendars together carry a powerful message of two people meeting, paths crossing, and fates intermingling: two separate paths through life have become in some way merged. Always bear days, dates and times in mind when interpreting a dream of this nature.

See also: CLOCK; CROSSROADS

CANDLE

If the three chief symbols of religion could be said to be faith, hope and love, a lighted candle represents hope, a reflection of the heart and its emotions.

If you see a lighted candle

This symbol is rather akin to the symbol of a light at the end of a tunnel: it expresses a glimmering of hope and expectation of better times to come. The imagery of a distant candle in a window guiding the traveller lost in the dark is a powerful one, however unrealistic it may be.

If you are lighting a candle in your dream

Sentiment is burning in your heart, and your emotions are reaching out towards some person or perhaps a worthy cause. In days of old, lighting a candle was a simple means of seeing in the dark, and though nowadays largely obsolete, as a dream image it can still imply inspiration or revelation, perhaps a new understanding. 'A candle in the wind' can be taken to mean one person's efforts when struggling against overwhelming odds, and this may be your own sentiment regarding your current position in life. On the other hand, a whole bank of candles, or candles floating on the water such as may be seen at some religious ceremonies, imply that you are not alone in your expression of hope, and that communal emotions are running very deeply.

See also: ALTAR; CARVINGS; STATUE

CAR *A personal means of travel*

If a car is your own normal means of travel

For many people the motorcar is an essential means of getting about, and driving everywhere is second nature to them, almost like an extension to their legs. This makes their car a very useful dream symbol, because anything that happens to the car, or obstructs its progress, or makes driving in the dream difficult, reflects what is happening to them in real life. It represents the progress of your own self through life, and very clearly expresses your hang-ups, your day-to-day problems, your indecisions and certainties. If you run off the road, have an accident, break down, or run out of fuel, any of these will very clearly relate to your own behaviour, your health, and general fortune. Your car may be humming along on a smooth clear road, or churning through the deep mud, avoiding potholes or edging its way over rocks. Sometimes you may find the road running out altogether, and you will know that your lifestyle is running into serious difficulties; a change of course will be essential for your own well-being.

If you have a passenger in your car

There may be real people known to you riding in your car – family perhaps, or friends – and in this case the dream is pointing out that their lives have been affected by you, making you to some extent responsible for them. However your passenger may be a somewhat obscure figure, and not someone known to you in waking life. If you are taking a policeman in your car, the dream is telling you that your present course of action is morally correct, but at the same time warning you that if you are tempted to cheat your own conscience in some way, you will not escape the consequences. Complete strangers featuring as passengers in a dream may be archetypes of the unconscious mind, parts of your own psyche representing your higher, intuitive self. In this case it is important to heed their advice if they have any to offer, and the dream needs interpreting very thoughtfully. If your dream passenger turns out to be someone frightening and undesirable, pay careful attention to this, too. It will be a part of your own psyche making its presence known.

If you are riding in someone else's car

If the driver is a real person already known to you, the implication is that you have become in some way dependent upon them in waking life. If the driver is completely unknown to you, take careful note of this person's characteristics. He or she may be an unfamiliar part of yourself, perhaps the persona, your 'social mask', which is dictating your progress through life at the expense of your real needs. It may be that you are trying to conceal some aspect of your own personality.

If you do not normally drive a car

Highways represent the main thoroughfares of life – the direction in which the vast majority of people are heading. If you feel yourself in some way out of place in this mainstream flow of life in the dream, the symbol is probably very accurately reflecting your own attitude to others. This is in itself is neither good nor bad. If you are struggling to make progress, constantly impeded by other people or their cars, perhaps you need to make an effort to fit in with the rest of the population. You may, however, be humming along very well without a car of your own, even outpacing everyone else, and the dream is drawing attention to the fact that you are not so materially orientated as the majority. In this case try not to lose touch with hard reality!

> *See also:* ACCIDENT; DRIVING; FLYING; JOURNEY; MUD; ROAD;

CARNIVAL   *A fantastic procession*

If you are taking part in the carnival

Carnival is a tradition which allows people to forget their problems, let their hair down and have a good time without too much responsibility. It represents a time when fantasy and sheer imagination is allowed to take precedence over boring day-to-day affairs, and moral restrictions are allowed to slip. The dream could be hinting that you have been ignoring your responsibilities and being a little selfish by putting your own pleasures first. But carnivals may appear to be more easy-going than they actually are; they need a great deal of preparation and dedicated energy, so are not really conducive to relaxation. You may be thinking of adopting a change of routine in real life that seems an easy option, but in practice it could well prove to be tough going.

If you are a bystander as a carnival goes past

Are you, the dreamer, looking disapprovingly as others enjoy themselves? Or perhaps you would like to join them if only you could? Whichever it is, the dream is reflecting the fact that you have been feeling left out of things in your waking life. It may be that you need to take a more lenient view of other people's behaviour, to relax a little and not take a strictly moralistic view all the time.

See also: MARKET; PROCESSIONS

CARVINGS   *Crafted objects made to represent someone or something*

The collective unconscious often makes use of dream symbols depicting carvings or figurines, often made of wood or ivory. They tend to represent something the dreamer would rather not identify or think about directly. They may carry the idea of ancient wisdom, or possibly superstitious beliefs that belong to the past. In effect they are 'symbols *of* symbols' that have been taken too literally in the past, and should now be seen for what they are. Quite often a dream carving can be understood as a phallic symbol referring to some sexual situation that the dreamer feels guilty about. They may have broader implications too, particularly if the carving is of some recognisable person, creature or thing. It may carry the implication of feeling restricted, of being obliged to accept a mere representation of something or someone the dreamer would love to know at firsthand. In ancient times carvings were thought misleading, or even wicked, because it was believed that naive people might worship them. This idea, long hidden in the collective unconscious, is at the root of the carving as a dream symbol. It represents something made by human hand that might take on an independent life, or an ability to influence, all of its own. Try to remember all the details of the dream carving to see if it will offer clues.

See also: IDOL; STATUE

CATHEDRAL   *A large and imposing church*

As a dream symbol, its meaning will largely depend upon the dreamer's own past experiences, and what the idea or sight of a cathedral brings to his or her mind during everyday life. There may be some particular association which springs to mind, and this of course will have a strong bearing upon the implications of the dream. Unlike churches, cathedrals tend to symbolise authority and establishment, the laws of morality and ritual. They are not as a rule cosy places where the ordinary church-goer can feel at home. They carry with them the air of special occasion and hierarchy, but are also very powerful symbols of devotion and a sense of awe. Following a dream involving a cathedral, careful note should be taken of the emotions which accompanied it, and they will provide a clue. As with most other dream symbols, if you have known a person who was closely associated with a particular cathedral in the past, this person could well have a bearing on the interpretation of your dream.

See also: ABBEY; ALTAR; CHURCH

CAVE   *A natural space or opening inside rock*

A cave can symbolise different things for different people, but it always refers in general to a hidden, secret place of concealment. It may be the dreamer's own unconscious mind where unwanted thoughts and impressions are stored. In waking life, a cave is hampering and restrictive, and not really suitable for a long-term stay. To find yourself inside a dream cave is to be enclosed or trapped within solid materiality, a place in the dark where the future is uncertain. As a symbol it could apply to your social situation, to your career, your health. It could be a temporary hiding place away from society, and imply that the dreamer is experiencing a period of depression.

If the cave seems a welcoming place

The dreamer may feel under threat in some way, and wishing to escape and be hidden from view. To a male dreamer, as a place of refuge a cave can symbolise his own mother, reflecting the idea of 'mother earth' – a place of safety where he could retreat as a child, but indicating the need in adulthood to break away from her dominating influence and claim true independence. Take careful note of the emotions associated with the dream cave, for these may provide a clue.

If the cave seems a threatening place

Some unknown danger may lurk in the cave – a distant folk memory of the Stone Age family seeking refuge and remaining watchful lest a cave bear should be inside: this is one possibility. Far more likely, though, the cave represents the dreamer's own personal unconscious mind, and the danger lurking inside is the dreamer's personal shadow. In this case the unknown horrors in the cave are already part of the dreamer's own psyche, and really need to become known. Once these deeply hidden contents are faced they will no longer represent a threat.

See also: ABYSS; ADVERSARY; CELLAR; DUNGEON; PIT; TUNNEL

CELLAR   *A basement or underground room*

In dreams, the 'self' is often seen as a house. It may be your own self, or somebody else known to you.The normal living quarters of this house represent those conscious parts of your mind which you normally experience, your everyday thoughts and feelings. The upstairs rooms or perhaps an attic represent the higher possibilities of your own psyche. The cellar which you rarely or never visit represents the unconscious part of your mind. If you consider the concept of yin and yang, the cellar is the yin, the dark, mysterious feminine place which receives and reformulates the impressions flowing from the conscious, male yang.

If you become aware of the cellar but do not enter it

This dream image implies that you would prefer not to meet the dark side of yourself: you feel the need to present yourself in the best possible light, and to keep certain aspects of your character hidden. You may have problems which you do not wish to face directly – problems which you should deal with before they become a burden to you.

If you enter the cellar in your dream

To analyse this symbol you need to remember all the details of your time in the dream cellar. What did you do there and what did you see? Or if it was too dark to see, what did you fear or suspect might be hiding there? The personal shadow lives in your dream cellar, composed of all the things about yourself that you have refused to accept as your own. If this dream figure were to emerge, he or she could prove quite horrifying, but it needs studying carefully if good is to come of it. Think round all the aspects very carefully.

See also: ABYSS; CAVE; DUNGEON; PIT

CHASING *Pursuing or being pursued*

If you are chasing someone in your dream

The dream symbol is fairly explicit: you are trying to capture something, achieve something which is eluding you. The question is: what? There will probably be other powerful clues in the dream which will help you identify the thing you are after, and possibly also tell you how best to go about securing it in real life. But of course, you may know who or what you are chasing in the dream. In this case the meaning should be fairly clear. You are after that elusive prize!

If you are being chased in your dream

This is a surprisingly common dream experience, because most of us normally try to avoid some confrontation or another, and symbolically run away from it. A dream symbol such as this is related to the symbol of the assailant, with perhaps a hint of the adversary. It may relate to some recent waking experience when you overstepped the mark in some way, and fear facing the consequences. If it is something deeper, hidden in the personal unconscious, you may not even want to identify it or find out its true nature – but if it continues to disturb your sleep, you really need to clear the matter up so that it can be expelled from your mind. The only sure way to find out the true nature of this dream pursuer is to allow it to catch you. After experiencing a dream of this sort, think round the characters and features of the dream very carefully. You may find you can 'ask yourself' for another dream of this nature so that you can allow the pursuer to catch you, and then see what happens. However, as this will give rise to a 'lucid dream' in which you are able to alter the action, take care you do not influence the outcome with your ordinary ego. Allow the dream to run its course.

See also: ESCAPING; FUGITIVE

CHILD   *A very young person older than a baby*

As with so many other dream symbols, the child in your dream may represent a real child, perhaps a family member or one with whom you come in contact. But in cryptic dreams the innocent child may be an archetype of the unconscious mind – an aspect of your personal unconscious mind – yourself as you would have been, if free from outside influences. The dream symbol of a young child may also represent something, some attribute or new idea, that has come to your awareness. You can be sure that a dream of this nature will be very important to you, psychologically and spiritually, and you need to analyse it very thoroughly.

See also: BABY

CHURCH   *A modest place of worship*

If the church is in use and flourishing

Your own normal understanding of a church and its functions will have a strong influence on the nature of the church as a dream symbol. At two extremes, some people look on 'church' with something approaching contempt; others think of it as something noble, a place of high aspiration. When attempting to interpret your dream involving a church, you will base your conclusions on your own preconceptions. At best, the dream church will carry a message of enhanced spiritual understanding and the path of submission to a higher will than your own. To dream of entering a beautiful church and feeling at peace implies just this. Unpleasant or disturbing dreams of church call for some honest self-appraisal. Other things related to church, such as towers, spires, singing choirs or pealing bells, can all carry much the same message as the body of a church itself.

If the dream church is ruined and abandoned

151

An ivy-covered ruin may seem romantic, but it carries with it powerful images of emotional certainties long gone. As a dream symbol a ruined church building tends to suggest an obsolete set of beliefs, or perhaps the feeling that spiritual revival has passed beyond recall. The dream may hark back to childhood, and may even represent a parent on whom you can no longer depend when in trouble. Your feelings may be sad and nostalgic, but the dream itself will probably indicate a new level of understanding, a new set of certainties coming to reality, not necessarily about religious matters. Very often the church symbol refers to human relationships which have become somewhat over-emotional.

See also: ABBEY; ALTAR; CATHEDRAL

CLIMBING   *Trying to achieve a higher position*

The track that you follow in your dream represents your own path through life, and if you are travelling along a steep section of that path, it can only mean that you are experiencing a difficult or frustrating period in real life. It may be of your own choosing, an attempt perhaps to reach a higher position in career or society.

If you dream you are in difficulties on your climb

You may seem in danger of falling or reach a point in your climb where you cannot go on. This is a warning symbol relating to your life: your own aspirations are leading you astray in some respect. You will probably know whether you seem to have taken a wrong turn in real life, and your everyday situation needs careful re-examination.

If you are climbing a mountain in your dream

As a rule, no-one *makes* you climb a mountain. It is a voluntary effort, and the same principle applies to climbing a dream mountain. The great majority of dreams involving climbing reflect

152

the dreamer's waking efforts to attain a better position, a better situation in life, the achievement of some ambition. It might relate to everyday life when this seems to involve heavy going: marriages sometimes seem like this, when you are making a big effort to accommodate someone else's feelings and needs. Gaining the top of a hill implies that things will soon get easier on the downhill slope. Ice and snow on the top reflect the fact that you seem to be experiencing an unrewarding phase of life, but again circumstances are liable to change soon and for the better. A mountain very obviously can symbolise a difficulty to be overcome in practical terms.

If you feel you are ascending a holy place

The symbol of climbing can also have a more spiritual meaning: the mountain may be purely abstract, and the act of climbing it will have significance only to the inner dimension, the soul. This is where the positive symbol of a mountain as a difficulty to be resolved becomes a negative one: if you are voluntarily climbing a mountain in your dream and you believe this to be a 'spiritual' symbol rather than a material one, you are probably climbing the wrong mountain! If you seem to be in danger of falling or sliding back down in your dream, take this as a gentle hint that you are tackling the subject in the wrong way. A 'spiritual mountain' simply cannot be climbed by effort of will, because desires of this sort belong to the material or occult and not the spiritual world. Your own experiences, hopes and fears in everyday life should make the meaning of your dream clear, and if this analysis still seems nonsensical to you, ask yourself for another dream that will make the matter plain. .

See also: LADDER; MOUNTAIN; OBSTACLES

CLOCK   *A timepiece*

A very telling symbol, which almost always relates to something very important in the dreamer's life. Time is a basic concept, an indication and a warning pointing to opportunities, consequences, trigger events, and fate itself. As a mandala, a clock can represent the dreamer's whole life, material, physical, psychological, and spiritual. There comes an important time in anyone's life when the fateful hour strikes, and all the dream details should be recalled and pondered over. Then again it could represent something that seems normal and everyday, like a time or date that should be remembered – an anniversary perhaps – and the dream is telling you that trouble lies ahead if you neglect to take the appropriate action. The substance of the dream clock may be significant: whether it is a rich antique, jewelled or made of gold, or perhaps plain and ordinary, or even rather cheap and nasty – these will be pointers to the 'quality of the moment' and the nature of the trigger that has prompted the dream.

If there are two clocks together in your dream

It is likely that one of those clocks represents yourself, the other symbolises some other person who is currently featuring strongly in your life. Two lines of fate have run together and could be pointing towards a single destiny. The meeting point is the trigger for a new start in life, a completely new direction. The dream needs analysing very thoughtfully to bring out its full meaning, an opportunity, so it seems, not to be missed.

See also: AUTUMN; CALENDAR; SUNDIAL

CLOTHES *Outward appearances displayed*

If your own clothes are in question

Our own clothes represent the way we present ourselves to the world, our persona, our own private disguise, our social facade, the way we think of ourselves and the way we think others may sum us up. It is quite common for people to dream that they are searching through their belongings to try to find the right clothes to wear, and finding nothing really suitable. A dream such as this implies that you are finding it difficult to fit in to the social scene, or whatever situation you find yourself in. Taking on new responsibilities for instance, facing up to problems, finding a new job perhaps: these are occasions when the dreamer may search in vain for the right clothes to wear. The symbol means you are lacking in confidence, worrying about whether or not you will fit in to the new situation, or what other people will think of you. Others tend to see you as you present yourself – your face value – and the way in which you project yourself is really up to you alone. We can only be really happy if we accept ourselves as we really are, but, society being what it is, we cannot always expect others to see it that way. Our dream clothes may also reflect our fears, sorrows and anxieties: a widow may dream of a black wedding dress; someone worried about illness may dream of discoloured or red clothes. It is a very personal symbol.

If you dream of other people's clothes

Like an actor's costume, clothes in a dream sum up the nature or character of the person wearing them. They represent the qualities and passions which you believe that person to possess. Important people, or higher archetypes of the unconscious mind in your dream may wear very impressive robes to stress the fact that what they have to offer may be of great value for your waking life. If the dream characters are real people known to you, their clothes will represent the way in which you think of them. If they are obviously imaginary or obscure characters, their clothes will symbolise the qualities or situations they are fulfilling in the dream.

See also: FASHIONS; HAT; NAKED

CLOUDS

Fog or mist seen in a dream show that the future, the physical or practical way ahead, is obscured and cannot yet be known by the dreamer. Clouds however, being normally above one's head, refer to a different dimension: they refer to an unknown situation that exists or may exist above the dreamer's knowledge, a higher status in psychological or even spiritual terms. If someone you know seems in a dream to have climbed or risen through clouds, the implication is that this person has attained a higher state that must remain unknown to the dreamer. Similarly, light billowing clouds seen in a dream express ideas that seem light and fantastic but may prove important in unforeseen ways. Clouds at night chasing across the moon may have romantic connotations, but they speak of changeability: you will not be able to rely on any new venture or relationship you have recently entered into. Dark storm clouds on the horizon have often been reported by dreamers who were shortly to experience troubled times, a fairly obvious premonition which may feature in a predictive dream, a warning dream, or a dream of the future.

See also: FOG; MIST

COCKEREL *A crowing rooster*

For thousands of years people have kept domestic poultry, and the crowing of a cock has become firmly entrenched as a symbol of new dawning – a wake-up call. It can also be a symbol of arrogance, or 'cockiness', of 'blowing one's own trumpet', the proverbial cock on the dunghill, lording it over his hens. It can also symbolise empty boasts, or even betrayal, as in the Christian story of Peter's thrice-denial of Jesus before cockcrow. In all cases the symbol represents a proclamation, an announcement of something that may be either good or bad. Your dream should tell you which: at best it may be the dawning of new possibilities, or at worst merely an empty boast on the dunghill of life.

See also: BIRDS

CORPSE   *Death*

If the corpse is of an unknown person

If no obvious meaning springs to mind, take note of whether the surroundings of the corpse in the dream were familiar to you, or if they represented an everyday situation for you. If so, the dream implies that something which you had, some abstract quality or line of business perhaps, is no longer available to you. If the surroundings are completely unfamiliar, the dream may be informing you that someone known to you is suffering a similar sense of loss. There are of course all sorts of circumstances by which you may be experiencing or fearing death on a day-to-day basis, and the meaning then will probably be only too plain.

If the corpse is of someone known to you

You may dream that someone close to you, perhaps a family member, lies dead, and this may reflect your fears and worries. It may be that you are being over-protective about this person. The implication may also be that the feelings of affection between you are effectively dead, and this will be a wholly personal matter. Very religious people may have this dream when they fear that the person concerned does not share their feelings of faith.

See also: BURIAL; DEATH; FUNERAL

COW   *Domestic cattle*

The cow is a powerfully significant symbol in many world cultures. It may reflect the world dream by symbolising the animal life forces as they relate to human beings. To a farmer, it may set the scene of a dream as reflecting an everyday situation. The symbol of a cow is liable to emerge from the collective unconscious as a representative of motherhood in the sense of a sustaining Mother Earth – the fertility goddess who is able to make

157

an appearance in many guises. It can represent pregnancy, or the wish to become pregnant. It can also represent gentle femininity, and is unlikely to refer to a woman in any derogatory sense. It should never be confused with the symbol of a bull, which carries a very different meaning.

See also: ANIMALS

CROCODILE   *A monstrous beast*

A frightening creature from the swamp – a crocodile, alligator, giant lizard, even a dinosaur – when it appears in your dream should seldom be taken at its face value. The chances are it will represent a part of yourself, coming to awareness perhaps from the personal unconscious mind, or the shadow. It will probably represent some characteristic, some set of emotions, that you had thought were long gone and forgotten; something perhaps that you would not wish to accept as part of your own nature. Dark desires that you try to suppress will lurk within the recesses of your unconscious mind, and build themselves up into this frightening form. The best way to deal with such a dream creature is to identify it and try to tame it in as harmless a manner as possible.

See also: DRAGON; MONSTER

CROSSROADS   *A choice of directions*

A fork in the road carries much the same implication, suggesting a moment of choice, a crucial stage when we are forced to make a major decision about the way our own life is going. A crossroads can also represent a meeting-point when two or more people or principles meet up together, a point at which they can react, join forces, or go their separate ways. There may be an element of doubt or hidden danger about the crossroads too, some 'dirty work at the crossroads'. Ideas of this nature are liable to appear as dream symbols when they reflect your current situation. When you are in doubt about which road to take, a helpful figure may well appear in your dream to point out the best route. When this happens, you should take careful note of the outcome, for it will probably be one of the archetypes of the unconscious mind, a wise person perhaps, who can give you excellent advice if your conscious mind is able to understand it.

See also: JUNCTION

CRYSTALS

Whatever crystals mean to you, this is probably the implication they will carry in your dream. Many people believe that crystals have special qualities of healing or even spiritual powers, and of course diamonds or other precious stones are also crystals. They certainly have value, but their value is a material rather than a spiritual one. If you feel very much attached to crystals in your dream, the message may be that you are putting your faith in the wrong direction, and ought to find out about your soul life – to look above material attachments and the values of this earth.

See also: EARTH; JEWELS

CUP   *A container to drink from*

The drinking utensil that features in your dream is a very basic symbol common to the whole human race. It draws attention to something that has entered or is about to enter the dreamer's waking life, some new understanding, some unforeseen twist of fate. Often, it represents an unpleasant duty or task that must be undertaken. The nature of the cup itself will give a hint as to the type of fate that is to befall. It may have a low and unpleasant nature, or it may equally be something of great and lasting value. It may perhaps have a misleading appearance of beauty while in fact containing something rather unpleasant to drink. There are many different slants which the cup may represent, and its meaning as a dream symbol will depend entirely on the dreamer's own experiences and expectations, and of course on any other incidents which feature in the dream.

See also: VASE; WATER

DAM *A great volume of water held back*

Water symbolises the emotions, the feelings, also the sexual desires. As a dream symbol the dam indicates that very powerful feelings are being held back and controlled – possibly by strength of will-power, by determination not to let your feelings show, perhaps by social or moral restrictions. There is plainly some good reason in waking life why these particular feelings should not be allowed to run free, but the situation could be a dangerous one. If the dam should burst, if you can hold back no longer, an uncontrollable flood of feelings will be released. This is the nature of dams: what should by nature be a steady trickle or smooth flow of water, is transformed into something potentially very powerful, something which could prove unstoppable. The dreamer will probably know what the dream is referring to. Perhaps a way can be found to release some of the water to avoid possible disaster.

See also: WATER

DANCE

There are basically two types of dance: those which stem from the inner feelings, and those which arise from the passions. You could say that the one is spontaneous while the other is contrived. To dance from the inner feelings in your dream is showing you that your dreaming self is not controlled by materiality, or by the desires.

160

If you are dancing alone in your dream

The everyday type of dancing in your dream will depend largely on your own experience and expectations of dancing in waking life. To dance on your own may indicate that you are keeping something secret from others, and warning you not to be too aloof. Perhaps you have been less than sincere with the people you normally mix with.

If you dream of dancing with others

To dance with another person in your dream usually indicates sexual desire for them which cannot be expressed in any other way. You may, of course, be a regular dancing partner and the dream is merely setting the scene with a situation that is familiar to you. Communal dancing, line dancing, square dancing, these may have a more subtle meaning in your dream. If the dancers form a square or circle this could be a mandala of your own self, and you need to study all the dream factors very thoughtfully.

See also: BALLET; THEATRE

DARKNESS

One normally sleeps in conditions of darkness, but when darkness features as a dream symbol it can prove rather frightening, with a sense of being lost, bewildered, and helpless. It implies that your way forward through life is being hampered and you cannot see what should be done. But, like night itself, darkness tends to be relieved after a while, and the dream may be telling you to have patience as the situation will soon improve. A particularly nightmarish dream of darkness, particularly when you cannot equate it to any real-life situation, can refer to the unknown part of your own self, the personal unconscious mind, and the darkest part of your own psyche, the personal shadow. This is waiting to be explored by you in your dreams, and the experience may prove of great value to your long-term psychological well-being. A dawn dream involving something frightening that seems to be emerging from the darkness needs careful consideration. The condition known as 'sleep paralysis' could be involved, when the difference between sleeping and waking during the hours of darkness becomes temporarily confused.

See also: ECLIPSE; LOST; TUNNEL

DARTS   *Aiming at a target*

Assuming you are not a great darts player in real life (in which case a game of darts may set the scene as a normal everyday experience), the dream symbol of throwing darts has a very clear meaning: you are aiming for a certain target which you may hit or miss in the dream. Your dream darts and dartboard may be referring to some specific aim, or they may be symbolising your efforts in life to achieve normal standards of living, expectations, social, moral or financial.

See also: DICE; PLAYING

DAWN   *Break of day*

Dreams about dawn

The end of a period of uncertainty and the dawning of new understanding. The full significance of this dream symbol will depend very much on individual experiences.

Dreams which occur at dawn

So-called great dreams arrive at or just before dawn, and are always of the utmost importance. For a full explanation, turn to pages 40 and 92.

DEATH

Death of a non-human

Powerful hopes and fears can trigger dreams, and the death in your dream may be a product of your everyday outward emotions being expressed in this way, rather in the manner of a wish-fulfilment dream, but with negative implications. But a dream arising from the inner feelings which portrays the death of some creature may be a reflection of the great world dream. A child may dream that an animal has died, and this will illustrate the fact that he or she is growing up in the normal way, and approaching the age of puberty.

Death of a human

In dreams the symbol of death may not refer to the death of the physical body. It is more likely to imply the "death" of some particular phase in your life, and points to new beginnings. It can also imply that some human faculty is no longer functioning as it should, and the other details of the dream need to be recalled and analysed carefully.

See also: BURIAL; CORPSE; DARKNESS; FUNERAL

DEMON   *A terrifying apparition in your dream*

What is a demon? Do they exist in fact? They certainly do in dreams, where a demon constitutes an archetype of the unconscious mind, and is one of the many forms which the personal shadow can take when it makes its presence known. It is made up of all the factors – thoughts, feelings, fears, faults and failings – which have been rejected or denied by the conscious mind. These factors do not exactly 'come back to haunt us' because they are already within our own psyche and have been there all the time, steadily consolidating and strengthening their nature beneath the surface of awareness until sooner or later they emerge in this frightening form. Any process of 'atonement', psychological or spiritual, will aim to tame and assimilate this symbolic figure.

See also: ADVERSARY; WITCH

DESERT *A barren inhospitable place*

The dream symbol of travelling through a barren place tends to reflect your own thoughts and feelings about your current life situation. Perhaps you feel powerless and undervalued, at a loss to know what can be done to better your position, and you feel your patience giving way to bouts of irritation and anger. The dream symbol itself is not hinting at what can be done to improve your lot, and you need to pay careful heed to any other features in the dream. If none of this applies to you, however, and your dream desert is insistent, it can only mean that your inner life is lacking some sort of spiritual contact. You need to seek to rectify this in waking life, and recording and paying heed to your dream-life is a move in the right direction.

See also: SAND

DICE

As a symbol of taking a gamble and resting in the hands of fate, rolling dice could scarcely be more explicit. As a dream symbol, it will probably relate to some circumstance of which the dreamer will be well aware . The numbers that come up may have their own significance, and again they will relate to the dreamer's own experience. We are all to some extent being swept along by the current of fate, and the hoped-for outcome may not be forthcoming. If you throw the double six in your dream this may be a wish fulfilment dream. If you have been fervently hoping for some particular outcome in real life, your own conscious ego may have intervened and tried to swing the dream hoping to influence events; it is unlikely to be a predictive dream of the future, even if you happen to be an inveterate gambler yourself.

See also: PLAYING

DIGGING *Penetrating the ground*

You may of course be a gardener or trench-digger in real life and the dream symbol is setting the scene as one with which you are familiar. More likely, though, it will relate to knowledge, some secret perhaps which you wish either to hide or to uncover.

If you are doing the digging

The symbol is probably referring to some mystery that has fascinated and baffled you in waking life. You may have forgotten something you thought vital and have been trying to remember it. In effect, you are trying to penetrate your own personal unconscious mind. Try to remember your feelings during the dream: were they feelings of hope, or anxiety? Were you trying to locate and uncover something of great value, or perhaps some guilty secret that has been worrying you? Perhaps you are searching for your own past, your roots? Only you can answer these questions.

If someone else is doing the digging

Again, your own feelings during the dream will give you a clue. If you are merely a spectator at the dig you are unlikely to be interested in somebody else's search for their own secrets. More likely, you believe that they are trying to uncover your secrets. Assuming you have not really buried a body in the back yard, you have perhaps been worrying lest people find out about something you would rather remained private. Is there a skeleton in your cupboard?

See also: ARCHEOLOGY; BURIAL; PIT

165

DIRT

It is natural for your personal unconscious mind to contain something akin to dirt, and your personal shadow in particular is made up of factors, feelings and ideas which you thought unworthy or disgusting and did not like to acknowledge as your own. A particularly moral person may feel that anything which does not conform to his or her ideas of morality is in some way dirty. The dirt which you dream about is more likely to have an abstract nature than to be real tangible dirt, and the other incidents in your dream should point to its nature. Dream dirt may be localized: you may have dabbled in something of which you are ashamed, and you will dream that your hands are dirty; you may feel aloof over some past fault or other which in fact is still influencing you, and you find that your feet are dirty. Others may have noticed the dirt and this may be embarrassing you in your dream. Take it as a gentle warning!

See also: EXCREMENT

DIVING   *Plunging into water*

The dream symbol of water refers to strong emotions and, it may be, sexual desires. Whether you are diving into water in the dream or whether you are merely watching others diving, the meaning is probably the same: 'taking the plunge' and committing yourself to these powerful passions. The dream itself should tell you whether the outcome will be good or bad, whether you should take the plunge or not. At this stage you cannot know what the outcome will be, but the practical wide-awake implications of the dream will probably be fairly obvious to you. Take special heed of any dream characters who appear. Are they real people known to you, or are they archetypes of the unconscious mind? Only you can decipher the full meaning of the dream and learn from it.

See also: WATER

166

DOCTOR

If the doctor in your dream is a real doctor known to you

The dream will probably be referring to a real medical problem which needs attention. If you have recently visited the doctor in real life, the dream may be telling you to think again about the diagnosis you received and the treatment you were prescribed: it may not be right for you and needs a rethink.

If the dream doctor is completely unknown to you

This could be an archetype of the unconscious mind conjured up by your inner feelings and ready to give you good advice, but the advice is more likely to be about psychological or spiritual matters than physical problems. Spiritual well-being is something that the outer personality does not really know about, but it is very real, and if any advice is on offer, we need to take it very seriously. Nowadays morality is often pushed out of sight, but it is important to the inner self, and your dream doctor may be referring to this side of the psyche when he gives advice. Your own feelings on waking, the theme mood of the dream, may give you an important clue.

> *See also:* BLOOD; HOSPITAL; WISE PERSON

DOG

Ancient symbol of the human-animal nature, dogs have been associating with people for thousands of years and fit in to our social systems very well. It is hardly surprising that they appear so regularly in our dreams. Referring to the world dream we can readily see that built into our own nature we have a certain affinity with the spiritual life-forces of the animal world. This affinity is likely to be portrayed by the dream symbol of the dog. In our dreams the personal shadow can take the form of a dog, often, perhaps, resembling our own familiar household pet, only to make its demonic nature known after it has been petted and accepted: a reminder that our psychic contents, both good and bad, are not always what they seem. You may, of course, dream of a real, friendly dog, or perhaps a savage one, and the dream itself will probably make its own meaning plain.

See also: ANIMALS; DEMON; WOLF

DOLL   *A lifelike toy*

The dream symbol of a doll is a remarkably personal one, and most difficult to penetrate by anyone other than the dreamer. It probably represents you, the dreamer, but in an objective way, as though you are standing back and observing yourself unfeelingly. What is happening to the doll in your dream? Who else is involved? Is it *your* doll, or does it belong to someone else? If you felt a strong emotion during or immediately after the dream, this will provide a valuable clue.

See also: STATUE; TOY

DOLPHINS

Creatures thoroughly at home in the sea: porpoises, probably seals and sea-lions too; we mostly think of them as playful and carefree, equally confident in rough seas or calm, supposedly intelligent and amazingly athletic. If they feature in a dream, they are probably referring to some group of people whom the dreamer admires, and whom he or she would rather like to join. But their social milieu is an unfamiliar one, and while they are masters of their environment they may not take kindly to intruders into their territory. Actual dolphins have an animal nature that can be cruel and uncaring as well as fun-loving and friendly. The dream could be a gentle warning to stick to the surroundings and company you know best.

See also: ANIMALS; WATER

DOOR

As a dream symbol, the difference between a door and an open entrance, or gateway, is that you cannot see through or beyond the solid door. You have no way of knowing exactly what lies on the other side. It may lead to a different level or state of being, a different lifestyle or cultural environment. The symbol of a door to be passed through often features in the dreams of those who have recently been bereaved, or in actual 'near-death' experiences. You may wish to go through the doorway but cannot, or perhaps you wake up before you can get through. Passing through an open doorway or a gate, on the other hand, usually refers to some new level of knowledge you wish to attain, and carries no hint of death. You know what is there and merely seek to attain it.

See also: GATEWAY

DRAGON

The mythological dragon is a guardian of the personal unconscious mind, however that concept might be expressed and described. Some cultures hold dragons in great esteem, and the people of these cultures tend to keep their own subconscious contents well hidden and unacknowledged. Other cultures may have a mythological tradition of having killed a dragon which was holding them in thrall, and these people are usually quick to acknowledge their own hidden contents and aim to bring them out into the open. A clash of cultures may well result, because these myths are more than mere imagination on the part of our ancestors. So the significance of a dragon which features in a dream will depend entirely on the dreamer's own cultural background. The dream dragon may be guarding a cave which probably holds a treasure, and this treasure amounts to the benefits that would ensue following the assimilation of one's own unconscious contents, resulting perhaps in a greater degree of psychic wholeness.

See also: ABYSS; CAVE; CROCODILE; MONSTER; TREASURE;

169

DRIVING *Being carried by your vehicle*

Driving a car is second nature to very many people, and as a dream symbol it represents one's personal progress through life. The car itself symbolises the solid materiality of the human body, and the road symbolises the progress of life and the incidents encountered along the way. For people who do not drive, much the same meaning is to be found in taking a bus or a train, riding a bicycle or a horse, or merely walking along the path. The incidents met with along the way, the state of the road, the behaviour of other road users, these will all need a strictly personal interpretation, for only the dreamer will know about the real-life things that have happened and are happening to him or her. To dream of carrying other people as passengers in your car suggests that the dreamer has or feels a certain responsibility towards them, particularly if they are members of the family or colleagues. Being driven by someone else implies the opposite: the dreamer is in some way reliant upon the person doing the driving.

See also: ACCIDENT; CAR; JOURNEY

DROWNING *Feeling helpless in deep water*

As a dream symbol deep water usually symbolises the great depth of your emotions, including your sexual feelings, and if you are out of your depth and in danger of drowning, the implication seems fairly obvious. Your emotions are becoming overpowering, and you need to step back and take an objective view of your life situation. If water is merely one symbol among many in the dream, and especially if there is a narrative, or series of dream incidents leading up to immersion in water or danger involving deep water, the dream will probably need personal interpretation, taking all the factors into careful consideration.

See also: TIDAL WAVE; WATER

DUNGEON   *A dark lock-up*

The dream dungeon is liable to be part of yourself – your own personal unconscious mind, in which case, anything it contains will belong to you. Your personal shadow may lurk inside your dream dungeon, and this frightening figure is composed of all the factors you have refused to face during your normal everyday life. If you are yourself a prisoner in the dream dungeon, the implication is that you are feeling trapped by your own contents. It would help you if you make an effort to explore the hidden side of your own personality, by thinking back through your life.

See also: CAVE; CELLAR; PIT

DUST   *fine dirt that has settled*

Dirt tends to be acquired from outside of your surroundings. Dust tends to be made up of fine particles eroded from those surroundings, and which have settled over the years. It may even originate from your own body, flakes of your own skin. Dream dust tends to imply that you have been neglecting everyday values, that you are becoming hide-bound, perhaps overlooking the things other people may find important. These factors need thinking round carefully. Dust builds up to the point where it may be difficult to breathe, and if you have experienced some real-life incident which involved lots of dust, this may well feature unpleasantly in your dreams. This is one type of situation where a lucid dream may be helpful, when you can make the dust blow away!

See also: BROOM; DIRT; EXCREMENT

EAGLE   *Large bird of prey*

A very ancient dream symbol, a pre-civilisation image of power, majesty, cruelty and wildness, supremacy, mastery of environment,

171

keen eyesight, and pride. A dream eagle may symbolise any of these things and more in an abstract sense, or perhaps a person who somewhat resembles an eagle in looks and characteristics, and the influence such a person may be having on the dreamer. In America the bald eagle in particular can symbolise patriotism and the quality of being American. All the supposed qualities possessed by large birds of prey may be represented by their appearance in a dream, but individually one's own ideas and experiences will decide the significance to be attached to a dream eagle.

See also: BIRDS

EARTH MOTHER *The world and its characteristics represented by a human-type figure*

A personification of the planet on which we all live, the concept of the Earth Mother is closely associated with the concept of the world dream. She is everybody's mother, and she nourishes and cares for us all; everybody will have their own image of her, hidden in their unconscious mind and liable to emerge in dreams when aroused by some trigger event. Despite her common inheritance, to become aware of this great supernatural mother goddess in dreams is a wholly personal event, and may reflect the beginning of the type of spiritual awareness that can mature into a quest for spiritual reality on a universal scale.

See also: GODDESS

EARTHQUAKE

When the familiar solid earth suddenly shakes, it shows that you can no longer rely on the stability of something you had thought unquestionably reliable. You may of course have experienced violent earthquakes yourself and the symbol will have become reality in your life; but if not, its meaning will be perfectly plain:

the only question is, what does the 'earth' represent to you? It could be your family, or your employment, or some institution on which you have relied, or society's attitude towards you personally, or your health, or wealth. If it is any of these things you will probably know the answer. If not, the shaking 'earth' might represent materiality itself: a dream earthquake could be hinting at the temporary nature of life, and the possibility of coming to spiritual awareness, to seek broader horizons and new worlds.

See also: VOLCANO

EATING

Anything you imbibe may be symbolised in a dream as eating; not only actual food, but information and impressions as well. If the dream is pointing out that you are taking something into yourself, it will probably refer to something previously unsuspected, and possibly something which may do you harm. If actual food is featured, try to identify this and think about it carefully: you may be making yourself ill by eating something that is bad for you: perhaps some of the ingredients or cooking methods need changing. But all the other features and characters in the dream need looking at very carefully: they may seem to have nothing to do with actual food but relate to influences that are affecting you negatively, which only you, the dreamer, can interpret.

See also: BREAD; FEAST; FOOD

ECHO

If your voice is echoing in the dream

In ancient Greek myth the nymph Echo fell in love with the vain youth Narcissus, and when she finally realized that he loved no-one but himself, she pined away until only her voice remained.

This is the prior meaning of an echo as a symbol: unrequited feelings, loneliness, a sense of hopelessness of purpose. Perhaps you are pitting yourself against an uncaring world, and the reply you hoped for does not seem to be forthcoming.

If the echo is caused by others

Memories lingering, the words remaining when the person has gone. If this featured in your dream, try to recall the emotions you felt at the time or on waking. Were these feelings pleasant or unpleasant? You may know who or what was the source of the echo. Are you echoing someone else's words, or trying to shake off the memories you would rather forget? Only you, the dreamer, can know the answer.

    See also: LOST

ECLIPSE   *The earth's shadow*

A solar eclipse

The sun must be one of the most ancient of symbols, the giver and keeper of life, the source of energy, and symbolic representative of spiritual powers. When the sun's light and heat is withdrawn, the implication is that some of these qualities are being withdrawn. Career prospects and financial affairs are symbolised by the sun, and the earth symbolises materiality and the burden of fate. When the earth's shadow covers the sun it suggests that one's source of income, comfort and security are in danger of being depleted in some way.

A lunar eclipse

The moon, an equally ancient symbol, is more personal than the sun, and relates to emotions and physical welfare. In a dream, when the earth's shadow falls across the moon giving it the dark reddish appearance of a lunar eclipse, romance and health are the probable issue. The dream may simply be expressing your own fears in these areas, but it may also carry the practical meaning of problems with the heart and circulation, or relating to the menstrual pause.

See also: DARKNESS; MOON; SUN

EGGS

A potent symbol of new life, of the imminent emergence of a new life form, of new growth, of the spring of the year, or of rebirth after death. They also symbolise sex as being at the root of all creation, and may represent erogenous zones of the human body when the dreamer does not wish to be more specific for whatever reason. To dream of broken eggs implies that the hoped-for outcome of an enterprise will not be forthcoming. As always, the full contents and context of a dream featuring eggs should be explored for personal meanings, and only the dreamer can do this successfully.

See also: EMBRYO

ELEPHANT

Usually amiable, potentially terribly dangerous; their great size and slow movements make them ponderous and impressive, rather like some official organizations. A dream elephant may well represent something like this, particularly if the dreamer has in some way fallen foul of authority. The elephant in your dream may also represent a person known to you – a caricature of somebody with rather similar characteristics.

See also: ANIMALS

EMBROIDERY *Fancy needlework, tapestry or stitch-craft*

If you are embroidering in the dream

In the same vein as painting a picture, you are creating something that is not really there, or is not necessarily exactly as you are depicting it. It could be that you are deceiving someone – probably without ill-intent – and 'embroidering the truth' a little to make it appear more acceptable. Perhaps you have been explaining something complicated, and this is how your dream represents it.

If the work has been done by someone else

The whole of nature has often been described as a 'tapestry' of innumerable life forms, and the dream image of a completed or half-formed tapestry could be expressing this, and the way in which you or something which has been occupying your attention fit into the scheme of things. Plainly a complicated situation is being symbolised. Could it be a 'tapestry of lies'?

See also: ART; PAINTING

EMBRYO

As a dream symbol this could be an unseen 'thing' about to emerge, or perhaps a chrysalis, or a hatching egg. The embryo is something new that is taking shape, whether it be solid and tangible or purely abstract, as an idea. Take careful note of your feelings when interpreting the dream, as these will give you an indication of whether the emergent entity is good or bad, wanted or unwanted.. The embryo itself may fail to develop and be aborted, and the implication is that an idea that may have seemed brilliant and promising has not fulfilled its promise.

See also: EGGS

176

ENEMY   *A cause for defensive action*

The term 'enemy' might cover many types of dream experience. We speak of an assailant when we mean somebody or something from outside of ourselves that seems to be opposing us in some way; and we speak of an adversary to mean a hidden part of our own psychic contents that has become personified as an opponent. An enemy may represent a real threat from a real person, or it too may be a personification of an inward problem that is becoming troublesome. It largely depends on the understanding of the person concerned, and the full context of the dream needs to be carefully analysed to find out what the problem is, and whether defensive action is required or if the problem lies in your own understanding of the situation.

See also: XENOPHOBIA

ESCAPING

If you are escaping in the dream

It is a fairly common dream experience, to be running away from something, someone, some kind of confrontation. If you are hiding from something, the cause needs to be identified and put into perspective. There may well be a real-life situation from which you feel the need to withdraw, and if this is the case the dream needs studying carefully to see if it contains any useful clues. If there is no obvious reason to escape, it may be that the dreamer is feeling stressed and could do with some time off, to 'get away from it all'.

If someone else is escaping from you

The symbol is certainly plain, and there should be a fairly obvious real-life situation which has triggered the dream. If there seems to be no such state of affairs, the escape has to be purely an abstract situation. It could be an outmoded or incorrect idea or attitude which you would be better off without. Why should anyone want to run away from you? the whole dream should provide the clue. You may have hurt someone's feelings inadvertently or upset someone's peace of mind.

See also: FUGITIVE

EXAMINATION   *Being tested for knowledge*

It is a fairly common dream experience, to approach some subject, some project needing your expertise, with confidence, only to find to your dismay that you know nothing about it and are unable to answer any questions. There may not be any parallel in real life that you can think of, but the dream will probably be referring to a completely abstract 'exam'. You have been over-confident, too sure that you know the answers, but in what context? A variation of this theme is to dream that you are about to deliver a lecture on some subject about which you are confident, only to discover too late that you know nothing about it. A careful analysis of all the dream details may provide the clue: it could be referring to work, or to marriage. Exams are personal, individual things. The dream could be telling you to share your confidences, confide your problems and your worries, and not try to take too many responsibilities on your own shoulders.

See also: JUDGE

EXCREMENT

Human excrement in a dream symbolises faults and undesirable features that you need get rid of. In fact, the implication is that these factors have already come out of your body – your mind, your psyche – but by the nature of excrement which clings where it touches, you may be finding it very difficult to discard these things completely. 'The sow that was washed rolls in the mud again', and, like a bad habit that will not go away, memories cling. The whole dream needs analysing very thoroughly for clues, and if you can identify the nature of the dream excrement you will certainly benefit from the knowledge. Animal excrement can feature in dreams too, and may be pointing out that your affections are being misplaced in some direction. Time to be realistic!

See also: DIRT; DUST; TOILET

FACADE   *A false front*

Buildings often have facades – a built-up front wall perhaps to make the place look more impressive, or to fit in better with its surroundings. In dreams a false front is more likely to be a personal matter involving the persona, and the self is often symbolised in dreams as a building of some sort. If the building represents a real person, the dream is showing you that the person is putting on a false front in public, and of course that person might be you! Sometimes the opposite is the case – a building (or a person) is made to look less impressive, less significant than it really is, camouflaged, a case perhaps of 'inverted snobbery'. In both cases the dream is telling the dreamer something that could be very useful to him or her. There are numerous permutations of this dream symbol, and your personal interpretation is essential.

See also: ACTING; ART; PAINTING; THEATRE

FACTORY   *A place where things are manufactured*

This dream symbol may of course refer to a real place of work and feature in an everyday dream, but on a larger scale it represents the power of materiality itself – the source of worldly wealth and normal social interaction.

If you dream you are outside of a factory looking in

There may be a theme mood that will give you a clue. When you saw the factory did you feel that it was a good place to be, or somewhere to be avoided? This will reflect your own current attitude towards the hurly-burly of everyday life: you might want to join it, or escape it. The dream is offering you a look into your own self. You may perhaps be lacking in social confidence, with a feeling of 'them and us' with yourself as the outsider.

If you are inside the factory and taking part

The dream factory may be an attractive place for you to be, or it may be somewhere you would dearly like to escape by retiring from the daily routine. This will reflect your attitude towards the society in which you live and work. Factories normally produce things: did these products feature strongly in the dream? They are the products of materiality, and if you found them unattractive in the dream, this could be reflecting your desire to seek a higher purpose in life.

See also: MACHINERY

FALLING

The sensation of falling is a common dream experience, sometimes happening without any dream images or symbols to support it. Some scientists suggest that the feeling harks back to the days when, like chimpanzees, humans made themselves sleeping-nests in trees, when falling was a very real danger. But the sensation always implies that the foundation or attitude of mind that you have been relying on is not quite so secure and solid as you had supposed. Usually, when we experience the sensation of falling, we wake up before we 'hit the bottom'. It would be interesting to stay asleep and experience the conclusion of the fall: whatever the outcome, it will already be a part of your own psyche and can do you no real harm. Identifying the nature and outcome of the fall may have lasting benefits on your waking life. You may of course dream of falling from a specific place, a bridge perhaps, or a high building, and this will need analysing accordingly.

See also: ABYSS; BRIDGE; CLIMBING; DIVING

FARM

A farm is a practical place where crops and animals are reared, and anyone with farming experience may dream of a farm as an everyday background to their dream incidents. A dream farm is a 'virtual place' where principles and soul-contents may be nurtured rather than anything with financial expectations. A dream baby may represent an aspect of the self coming newly to awareness, and a dream farm may represent the place where this child of the psyche is being reared: in other words, the farm can be a symbol of your own self. If this is the case in your own dream, try to recall any features and characters connected with the farm: they may represent important aspects of your own inner self which ought to be acknowledged.

See also: ANIMALS; CHILD; ZOO

FASHIONS   *To follow the current trends*

Style of clothes

As a dream symbol your clothes represent your outward personality and the impression you give or would like to give to others. In everyday life you tend to wear the same as others of your set, or perhaps people you admire, or young people, or forward-looking people: you are trying to be accepted as one of them and do not wish to stand out as different. Perhaps in your dream you are admiring the fashions of others but cannot match them, and the implication is that you are falling short of the ideal, in your own eyes at least. Or you may see the other dream characters as slaves

181

to fashion and you are proud to be different in this respect, and this will reflect your attitude in real life: you refuse to go along with the crowd and prefer to think of yourself as individually unique.

Fashions in other respects

Fashions change continually, reflecting the normal tastes of the day. Perhaps you fear appearing old-fashioned, or possibly you want to stay out of the rat-race and refuse to go along with the latest gimmicks. In either case what happens in your dreams reflects your feelings in real life. You may be gazing wistfully at the possessions and lifestyles of others, and feeling left out of things; or perhaps you may be constantly involved in a race to 'keep up with the Joneses'. Dreams of this nature quite accurately portray your position in society as it is, and as you would like it to be.

See also: HAT; NAKED; UNIFORM

FEAST   *A celebration with eating*

Ordinary food or the mere act of eating is a dream symbol of taking in – and it may refer to information, impressions, learning, mental or even spiritual sustenance rather than actual food – but feasting certainly implies a degree of self-indulgence. The details of the dream are important, and so are the emotions which you may have felt during the dream or immediately after waking. If you felt rather guilty during your feast, perhaps you are being greedy or selfish in some respect. But if you felt only pleasure, and particularly if others were sharing your feast. it could be that you are set to receive some good fortune or a happy occasion, perhaps a family reunion.

See also: BREAD

FEET

Rather like driving a car, feet symbolise one's progress through life, and the state of your feet in the dream may carry implications about your own attitude, your relationship with others, and the problems you encounter along the way. To dream you have deformed or damaged feet implies that you are experiencing difficulties in the normal course of events, but feet usually have a spiritual connotation in a dream: the journey they symbolise is the march towards psychic wholeness which is represented in numerous different ways both in psychoanalysis and in the religions of the world. To understand the importance of this symbol is an important step along this path. If the dream carries a hint of 'treading on somebody's toes' or harming others in some way, take it as a stern warning to live and let live. Studying and recording your dreams in detail is one way to become more aware of life's spiritual journey.

See also: PATH; LAMENESS; ROAD

FENCE *A wooden or temporary barrier*

A dream fence is less final, less impelling, than a wall. Both are barriers, but you can often see through a fence whilst a wall is solid and hides what is beyond it. The barrier may be physical, mental, moral, psychological, or spiritual, but you can usually 'see' beyond the barrier and understand what lies beyond it. The fence may be there for your own good, certainly for your own guidance, and it may direct you towards a safer path. To dream that a fence has fallen or blown down implies that a way which was formerly closed to you has now been opened. Simple analysis of the dream symbol is easy; only the dreamer personally can interpret the full meaning of the dream.

See also: GATEWAY; HEDGE; WALL

183

FISH or FISHING

The collective unconscious has often been described as a vast sea full of archetypal images, and it is quite understandable that the desires, hopes and fears of the human race are often symbolised as creatures which live in this largely unexplored sea, for once these things enter the unconscious part of the mind, by definition they will have disappeared from consciousness, but still they live on, unseen and usually unsuspected. This is not merely an imaginative way to speak of forgotten matters that may suddenly be recalled to mind: it is much deeper and more significant than that. On a more personal scale the sea may symbolise one's depths of emotion, including sexual feelings. So may a lake, a river or a brook, and the creatures which live in it will be the emotional matters that we do not wish to recall, perhaps things we felt guilty about, or found too disturbing even to ponder. The dream image of fishing – either by you personally, or as a spectator – expresses your own wish to enter this unconscious world, to uncover your own contents, and set out on a journey, both psychological and spiritual, which will change your life for ever. On a more practical level, perhaps, it can symbolise a wish to uncover your past, particularly if you have recently acquired an interest in your ancestry and family history.

See also: ANIMALS; SEA; WATER

FLOWER

This is a multi-faceted symbol when it appears in a dream, as it can refer to several different principles. The whole dream needs analysing very thoroughly: are the dream flowers real flowers, or archetypal ones? If real ones, there may have been trigger events recently. In archetypal terms the persona or social mask that you wear can be dreamed of as a flower, or a vase of flowers, because obviously you want to be seen as an attractive person. A solitary flower can be a mandala of the self – a picture perhaps of your own soul. A flower such as a water lily floating on water can symbolise your own self – your conscious self growing above the unfathomable contents of the unconscious mind. Emotional and sexual encounters may be symbolised by beautiful and exotic flowers, while flower-grown meadows often feature in 'death' dreams of the afterlife. On a more down-to-earth level, faded flowers may represent unfulfilled hopes and disappointments, while flourishing blooms express the hope of good times ahead.

See also: FOREST; LILIES

FLYING *To dream that you are flying in the air*

As a rule dream images are selected and presented by the inner feelings, and these hidden feelings, also known as the 'higher emotional centre', are not bound by materiality or by the physical body. There is nothing to stop them flying around freely, and time and space are no real barriers to them. It sometimes happens that in your dream you seem to have two bodies, one heavy and earth-bound, the other light and able to fly: this is the distinction between these two modes of feeling, the material and the non-material. Ordinary dreams of flying in a plane, or perhaps hang-gliding and looking down over the world, can reflect a feeling of superiority, and this superiority may be either real or purely 'wishful'. Airliners in a dream are likely to carry the practical significance of travel, perhaps of someone or something having just arrived into your awareness.

See also: GLIDER

FOG *Heavy mist obscuring your view*

When a situation is uncertain and rather worrying, your dreams are likely to involve mist or fog to represent these negative feelings. The implication is that you cannot see any better way forward at present, and patience is necessary. Real fog often accumulates in low-lying place such as valleys, and the valley itself will represent the material situation that you find yourself in – your circumstances, your health, your career prospects. It also accumulates over water, and this fog may be referring to your emotional problems and your sex-life. Real fog lifts before long, and the implication of the dream may be that although you cannot see your way ahead clearly, the situation should improve before long. Sometimes you may dream you are standing on a hill and looking down at heavy fog or mist covering the plain and valleys beneath, and the implication seems to be that you have risen above your difficulties and should find a clear way ahead in future.

See also: CLOUDS; MIST; VALLEY

FOOD

The thoughts and impressions of the day are food for the unconscious mind to be digested through the night. Symbolically, all influences and any piece of information can be seen as food for the mind, for the emotions, for the psyche. In dreams there are endless permutations of the way in which abstract matters can be seen as food, and these possibilities need to be borne in mind when analysing dreams involving food. But of course the dream image of food can have a purely practical meaning too, particularly if you dream you are eating bad or stale food. This may be literally true if you are inadvertently using food that is bad for you.

See also: BREAD; FEAST; FRUIT

FORD   *A shallow river crossing*

In dreams a river or a stream symbolises the flow of emotions, including the sexual desires, and these psychological forces can seem overpowering. You may be happy to swim in the river, to submerse yourself in the current of feelings; you may wish to keep aloof from these things during some encounter in your life, and you will look for a bridge enabling you to cross safely; but you may wish to 'test the water', to paddle through the river sampling the experience without becoming too involved, and a ford will symbolise this. If you are following a spiritual path you will sooner or later need to cross the dream river to become independent of these potent life forces.

See also: BRIDGE; PATH; RIVER; ROAD; WATER

FOREST

You may of course live in a forest, or have a background of forest life, and to dream of a forest may be simply setting the scene for you. But if not, a dream forest usually symbolises the mind – the 'forest of the mind' – when your thoughts are keeping you from seeing broader possibilities. The world with all its opportunities is, of course, not confined to your own ideas, your own preconceptions, and to walk through a dream forest seems to be telling you to look beyond the trees, to quieten your own thoughts and look for opportunities that may not seem logical or scientific. Many great thinkers are hampered by their own power of reason which can shut off higher possibilities for them, and they are then apt to dream of walking through a forest. In the world dream too forests are significant, and tend to represent aggression and the search for power.

See also: AUTUMN; HEDGE

FORTRESS

If you are outside the fortress trying to get in

A fortress represents security – or apparent security – and if you are trying to get in, plainly you are searching for security in one way or another. Marriage is often symbolised in dreams by a

187

fortress, or a strong tower, and this may be the implication in your dream. You will probably be feeling weak and helpless and insecure while you remain outside the fortress, unable to get in. A fortress may also symbolise your family, or some organisation you were hoping to join. Remember if any person known to you in waking life featured in the dream, for the identity of that person will provide the key.

If you are inside the fortress, looking out

All the features that tend to isolate the individual can be symbolised by a fortress, and it may be that you the dreamer have been feeling unsociable for whatever reason. You may suspect danger outside and are clinging to the security of your 'fortress'; or you may perhaps feel trapped in the fortress and would like to escape. If you can recall any strong emotion in the dream this will help your interpretation. It is an unequivocal symbol and the dreamer will probably know what it means and what needs to be done about it.

See also: BATTLEMENTS; FUGITIVE; TOWER

FOSSILS   *Ancient remains of once-living creatures*

Ancient life-forms that no longer live but have come to light unexpectedly. Past thoughts and impressions that were rejected and forgotten but have suddenly come to the awareness again – your inner feelings may have made this connection in your dream. Whatever else follows the discovery of a fossil in your dream will probably recapture the 'meat' of that long-dead creature, and the long-forgotten ideas, impressions or information that were relegated to the unconscious mind. These things will not simply disappear, and need your waking attention.

See also: ANTIQUE; ARCHEOLOGY;

188

FOUNTAIN or SPRING

The ancient symbol of water gushing out of the ground signifies something new which has come to awareness, a new source of knowledge, or an unsuspected reason to feel great emotion, or perhaps a new surge of sexual attraction. It could relate to new birth, or a new and exciting discovery relating to society, business, religion, art or music. It is such a clear symbol that the dreamer will probably know immediately to what it refers.

See also: WATER

FROST

The atmosphere is our natural environment, and water symbolises emotions: water in the atmosphere or dew which has frozen implies that your emotional surroundings and thence the attitudes of other people towards you have become distinctly frosty. There may be a good reason for this – only you, the dreamer, can know. There may be a difficult, slippery path to follow for a time. But the nature of frost is transient, and conditions should improve eventually.

See also: GLACIER; SNOW AND ICE; WATER

FRUIT

The outcome of something is often symbolised by fruit: your new enterprise: will it 'bear fruit'? Your children, the 'fruit of your loins', will they achieve attractive ripeness, or shrivel up and wither? When they feature in a dream, fruits, and your children too, may symbolise your own ideas, hopes and ambitions. Fruit can also symbolise health, or healthy relations with others, particularly in physical terms. Things that have the appearance of fruit in some way, if they are attractive to the dreamer, can also feature in dreams as actual fruits, frequently with a sexual connotation.

See also: FOOD

189

FUGITIVE   *The outsider escaping or hiding*

Assuming that the dreamer has no real-life practical reason to evade capture and the dream is reflecting this situation, and possibly offering helpful clues, the symbol of running away, or of gazing wistfully and longing to join society, is very expressive of the desire to achieve a more rewarding lifestyle. The implication is that the dreamer has been feeling left out of things, and would dearly like to be accepted on more equal terms. The context of this dream symbol will be entirely a private matter for the dreamer. This is one of those symbols which offers easy analysis without knowing the background facts, but only the dreamer personally has the inside knowledge to be able to interpret it successfully.

See also: ESCAPING; LOST

FUNERAL

Waking thoughts and fears of death may well produce a dream funeral. The symbol is not usually to be taken literally, however. The implication of a funeral is that some symbolic 'life' has come to an end, and this 'life' may be a purely abstract principle: one of work, society, or a particular line of interest which is now over, a habit which has gone, or a friendship which has been lost. The end of a bad period is the necessary precursor of better times ahead. The past has to be buried before a new era can begin.

See also: BURIAL; DEATH

GATEWAY   *A way through that is not a door*

A door is a solid barrier that may be either open or closed. A dream gate is also a way through, and it may be closed, but you can see through it and in that sense you know what lies beyond it. You may wish to go through the gate; you may actually pass through it; or you may be aware of its presence but have no wish to go through to whatever you believe to be on the other side. As a dream symbol the act of passing through a gateway implies gaining a new way of thinking or looking or understanding.You have the desire and probably the chance to enter into a new phase of life, a new career or set of associations.

See also: DOOR; FENCE; HEDGE; WALL

GHOST

An unseen or nebulous presence in a dream implies just that: something you suspect might have an effect on you; something that you cannot put your finger on. You are probably rather scared of its possibilities should it become solid and tangible. It may be allied to the principle of a 'skeleton in the cupboard', perhaps a family secret that you do not want to be made known. If you believe that a ghost lurks in an unseen place – perhaps in a cellar – the dream symbol is hinting at something, some problem or hidden characteristic perhaps, that is threatening to emerge from the recesses of your personal unconscious mind. A dream ghost is something at least half hidden, that you would prefer to remain out of sight.

See also: ADVERSARY; DEMON;

GIFT

If you are offering someone a gift in your dream

Unless it has a specific meaning to the dreamer, your gift can be a representation of the *persona*. The implication is that you are offering an aspect of yourself to the other person, something that represents the way you would like them to see you. You may know the other person in real life, and their reaction to the gift will be very significant: they may be accepting or rejecting your friendship, your advice, your own opinion of yourself.

If you are being offered the gift

If the donor is known to you in waking life, the dream symbol should be plain. They are offering you something, not necessarily a material object, that may be of value to you, or it may be disappointing and rather unpleasant. Another person's advice tends to have this nature. The implication is the same if the dream character offering the gift is unknown to you: he or she may be an archetype of the unconscious mind. If this is the case the dream gift will probably be of great value to you. This is an interesting dream symbol, but a wholly personal one.

See also: ARCHETYPES; TREASURE

GLACIER

A solid, frozen river of ice: a dream symbol that probably reflects your own emotional attitude to others. Water in a dream usually represents the felings, or perhaps the sexual desires. Your emotions ought to be flowing freely, and your personal relationships should not be frigid. The symbol may also reflect the feelings of someone else close to you, in which case the outlook for future relationships is not good. There needs to be a warming of hearts on one or both sides of any partnership.

See also: FROST; SNOW AND ICE

GLIDER *Soaring above the ground*

You may be in the glider and looking down, or you may be on the ground and looking up at it. The former represents your own feelings experiencing a 'high', and the latter expresses the wish to leave earthly worries behind and float above them. In both cases, though the glider seems to be independent and free from the earth, and by implication free from all the responsibilities of earthly life, in fact it is still bound by the laws of gravity – the life forces of materiality – and has to come down sooner or later. It may be a wish fulfilment dream in which the dreamer seeks to escape the bonds of society, work, and responsibilities.

See also: FLYING;

GODDESS

What exactly is a goddess, and what does one look like? The answer depends entirely on the dreamer's own understanding. He or she will know if the dream figure is truly a 'goddess'. She may be the earth mother herself, and one of the archetypes of the unconscious mind, but she will certainly have emerged from the personal unconscious mind of the dreamer. She may offer sound advice when it is most needed, or she may provide a first inkling of the true nature of the world dream. Purely on a psychological (that is, not a spiritual) level, a dream goddess can personify the principle of female confidence and power, and the dream details should make the meaning clear.

See also: WISE PERSON; WITCH

GOLD

As the major symbol of wealth, gold can have two distinct and very different meanings: it can refer to the gold of the earth and material riches; or it may refer to spiritual wealth. In dreams, important people may sometimes be identified by their golden robes, and this often applies to archetypes of the unconscious mind when they appear in dreams ready to give good advice. To dream of finding gold or similar treasures is not always a good omen; it may refer to short-term gain leading to long-term disappointment.

See also: TREASURE

GORGE   *A deep cleft through solid rock*

If in your dream you are looking down at a gorge, a gulch, or a ravine

Solid earth and rocks form a very basic dream symbol referring to the strength of materiality itself, and a cleft in that solidity which you cannot or do not wish to enter is normally a symbol of one's own unconscious mind. If you fear falling in however, the implication could be a very practical one: you may be feeling in danger of losing security in some sense; losing your job perhaps, or feeling that your marriage is in jeopardy. It implies that materiality is not as reliable as you have thought.

If in your dream you are inside and exploring the gorge

Perhaps you are trying to find a way out. This implies that you are feeling hemmed in by circumstances beyond your control. The dream image may be warning you to withdraw from a situation before it is too late. The gorge could represent the recesses of your personal unconscious mind, particularly if you find yourself remembering disturbing images from the past which are liable to cause you problems. The gorge can also represent the female element of marriage when this is threatening to become overpowering in some way. On the other hand it may be that someone known to you in waking life has been exerting an unpleasant influence, and you need to appraise your current lifestyle very thoughtfully.

See also: ABYSS; PIT

GRAVE

The dreamer will know if this is a straight-forward reference to a real grave. If it is plainly not, as a dream symbol it will be pointing out the final outcome of a situation – a relationship, an enterprise, a way of life. It may well represent an emotional aspect in the dreamer's life that has reached its logical conclusion and needs putting to rest. The grave can also represent the recesses of the personal unconscious mind with its hidden contents – drawing attention to something that needs bringing out into the light: a guilty secret perhaps?

See also: BURIAL; DEATH; FUNERAL

HAT

The dream symbol of hats as worn by characters in a dream, or the dreamer personally, is closely allied to the symbol of clothes. They both express the nature and personality of the people wearing them, and their practical relationship to the dreamer. This is true whether the dream characters are real people known to the dreamer, or archetypes of the unconscious mind. In the case of the former, a hat might also represent the way in which the person would *like* to be seen, that is, their persona. When the character wearing the hat is female, it is worth bearing in mind that in some cultures and religions, a woman is expected to wear a head-covering if she is not to be thought wanton or immoral. In this case a hat may be a symbol of virtue.

See also: FASHIONS

HEDGE   *A barrier formed of living plants*

In effect, a narrow strip of woodland which encloses or divides or connects, forming a home for small creatures and a barrier for large ones, including humans. A dream hedge could be bearing flowers, a friendly hedge that will protect and guide your path; or it could be menacing, full of thorns, and a hindrance to your course through life. The world dream points out that plants may well symbolise aggression and struggle; but of course, on the face of it, they are

are also peaceful, beautiful and useful. One cannot be dogmatic about the hedge as a dream symbol; your dream will tell you which role it is playing, and you will interpret it accordingly.

See also: FENCE; WALL

HERO *A dream character who may solve your problems*

The hero-figure in a dream is closely allied to the wise person and the king, all archetypes of the unconscious mind who are really able to give you good advice, if you are willing to listen. They are interested in your problems, because they are part of your psyche – the highest part – and whatever your current course in life they can give a helping hand if you become aware of your dream life. This archetypal figure will not have an identity that he makes known to you, because he will remain a part of your unconscious mind. The hero figure in your dream may, of course, be a real person known to you, and on whom you have been relying, and in this case his help may not be as useful as you had hoped.

See also: KING; QUEEN; WISE PERSON

HOLLY

A holly hedge, like a hedge of thorns, can provide a formidable barrier – a thorny problem – but holly has the added dimensions of colourful berry, modest white flower, and festive associations. Holly sometimes appears in a dream when a new enterprise is under consideration, and the implication is that, though rewards should follow, difficult circumstances will be very much to the fore. Holly is a cautionary symbol: something that appears very attractive and useful, but also a warning that someone could get hurt.

See also: HEDGE; THORN

HONEY

Since ancient times honey has been greatly valued as a luxury food to be obtained at some personal risk. As a dream symbol a wild bees' nest or a beehive or a honeycomb carries this message: some advantage is to be gained if one is willing to take the risk involved. The expression 'a taste of honey' also has the implication of some kind of illicit pleasure indulged in against your better judgement. A pot of honey in these modern times will probably have lost its 'sting' as a dream symbol, and for anyone who is not a bee-keeper will simply point to a sweet situation. The word 'honey' of course is often used as a term of affection with no connotation of danger: the connection between honey and bees in this case has probably been lost over the years.

See also: FOOD; INSECTS

HORSE

Horses feature in dreams surprisingly frequently, even when the dreamer has no connection with horses personally. If that connection is there, the dream horse will have a practical meaning, but if not, there is usually a sexual implication. A white horse may represent a person whom you trust, but whose sexuality you are nervous about. A black horse may symbolise the sexuality of a person you find somewhat frightening: an unknown quantity; a 'dark horse'. If you are used to riding horses you will very likely be doing just that with the horse in your dream. Animal energy and stamina with great sexual capacity, naturally competitive, sometimes compliant, sometimes wild and untamed: there is always a powerful emotional overtone in dreams about horses. A unicorn, a horse with something extra, a horn, or perhaps a crown, expresses a spiritual element in addition to the more obvious sexual symbolism.

See also: ANIMALS

HOTEL   *A place where you or others are being looked after*

A dream hotel is not necessarily a real building: it probably represents some set of circumstances, or the surroundings on which you have been relying. It might be an organization to which you belong, or a family environment, or a safe haven of some kind. You will probably already be aware of or at least suspect the real nature of the 'hotel' which featured in your dream. It is quite a common dream circumstance to leave your 'hotel' and walk or drive away, only to find that you have become lost and caught up in unpleasant circumstances. This could be construed as a warning not to abandon some situation that has been beneficial to you, not to forget the principles you used to rely on.

> *See also:*   FARM; FUGITIVE

HURRICANE   *A cyclone, gale, storm, tempest, typhoon, or whirlwind*

Just as a real storm disrupts the elements and causes damage, a storm in the dreamer's own psyche causes disruption and possible emotional trauma. The cause may well be known to the dreamer; there may have been a series of trigger events, upsets in the family or at work. If there are no obvious clues that the dreamer can remember, this could be taken as a warning dream. It might refer to emotional upsets, possibly with a medical basis, that are due to affect either the dreamer personally or someone close to them. It may be referring to public reactions to something the dreamer or a member of the family has brought about, especially if that person is already in the public eye. Of course, the possibility of a real hurricane happening should not be ruled out.

> *See also:*   BAMBOO; EARTHQUAKE; TIDAL WAVE; VOLCANO

HUT   A *small building, a shed or shack*

Dream buildings often symbolise the self, and a small wooden building, a temporary shed scarcely large enough to hold more than one person at a time, tends to represent the individual who has become cut off emotionally in some way. If a person enters the hut in your dream, he or she is undergoing something that applies to them alone: they are on their own in every sense. It is quite often the symbol of illness or death. When the person emerges from the hut he or she will have become changed, and must seek or be shown a new direction, a new environment – for better or worse.

See also: BARN; DOOR

IDOL   *A symbol of something that is worshipped*

An idol symbolises a principle that is greater than either itself or its worshippers. As a dream symbol its meaning is bound to be wholly personal: what does it mean to you, the dreamer? What were your feelings during or immediately after the dream? Of reverence, or contempt, or fear? Did it feature strongly in a major dream, particularly a dawn dream? You need to explore your own feelings and understanding very carefully and sincerely. It could represent a step up for the dreamer, or a denunciation of something the dreamer was relying on, a letdown for the emotions. This is a very important dream symbol, and it needs thinking round very thoroughly.

See also: CARVINGS; STATUE

INCENSE

Religion, it has to be said, belongs to the heart. Spirituality belongs to the soul. When you first enter a truly spiritual path you may well experience ethereal incense – a non-physical smell that arises when coarse material characteristics are being expelled from the inner feelings. Many years ago the process was thought of as 'casting out demons', and people tried to recapture this experience by burning various substances that they thought recalled the supernatural smell, and this is why incense is sometimes burnt during religious ceremonies. If the smell of incense features in a dream, depending on the other dream features, it implies that the dreamer or the characters using the incense are exercising faith and sincerity; anything to be understood from such a dream should be valued and respected.

See also: CHURCH

INSECTS   *Running, crawling, creeping or flying bugs*

As distinct from parasitic bugs, the general term 'insects' covers a multitude of life-forms, including such creatures as spiders, which are not really insects at all. As a dream symbol, their meaning depends on what 'insects' mean to you personally. Some people find them repulsive; others take an interest in their lives and habits. If the former, they may reflect a problem of health and hygiene which you suspect exists, or perhaps a feeling of compromised security, when insects are getting in to your house. Any other clues in the dream need to be studied very carefully, because action on your part is probably urgently needed.

See also: ADVERSARY; ASSAILANT; BUGS

JETTY   *An inroad into the sea*

Access to the sea of emotion, or sexual desire, ready to board a boat to cross it safely, or perhaps to become washed away and lost in the flood: this is the implication of a dream jetty, a pier, a breakwater, or a causeway leading across the bay. The dreamer seems to be approaching a situation where these powerful feelings are rampant, and cannot decide whether to take part in them, to merely watch and wait, or to remain aloof without actually becoming involved. The sea always contains an element of danger, and it as well to identify your own dream sea, and the jetty which at present is supporting you. They will be very significant factors in your life.

See also: STEPPING STONES; WATER

JEWELS

Pearls which feature in a dream, in my experience, always symbolise a non-material treasure; gold can be either material or non-material; jewels or precious stones which have their origin in the ground almost always symbolise riches or advantages in a materialistic rather than non-material or spiritual sense. To dream you have access to a treasure-house may symbolise an upturn in business affairs.

See also: CRYSTALS; GOLD; PEARL; TREASURE

JOURNEY

If it is you taking a journey

The chances are your dream journey will probably refer to your normal progress through life, and will be pointing out and isolating incidents which happen to you along the way. Assuming you are not due to take a real-life journey, you can be sure it is an ongoing journey of the mind. Details may refer to your health, your work, your family relationships, and if it is possible to assemble the details of your dream journey in sequence, the resulting analysis will certainly prove revealing.

If someone else is going on or arriving from a journey in the dream

The chances are that this dream is predicting events that will coincide with these people coming to your attention in real life. Remember the details and await results over the next few days.

See also: CAR; FEET; PATH; RAIL JOURNEY; ROAD

JUDGE

If you are making a judgment in the dream

It is always easy to judge somebody else's words and deeds, because everyone falls short of perfection. But the religious injunction to 'judge not lest ye be judged' is something to be taken seriously, because everything you do is recorded by your own conscience – your own inner feelings – and your own soul, and sooner or later we all have to face the consequences. A dream of casting judgment would seem to be drawing attention to your own conscience and warning you to have an open mind.

If another person is sitting in judgment in your dream

If you are being judged in a dream the implication is that you are already feeling guilty about something you have done, either by word or deed. Your inner feelings are the seat of conscience, and they are telling your waking mind to be more careful in what you do or say; don't forget that words can be very hurtful, and inflicting injuries of this nature adds to your own burden in the form of your shadow which may cause completely unforeseen problems.

See also: ANGEL; EXAMINATION

JUNCTION   *A dividing of the ways*

A dream which seems to offer you the choice of directions in your path through life will certainly be reflecting your real-life situation, either physically, mentally or emotionally. Like a crossroads, a dream junction shows that your present course cannot continue, and a change of attitude must be made. A point of decision featuring in your dream often announces the appearance of an unknown character who turns out to be one of the archetypes of the unconscious mind. If this seems to be the case on waking, all the dream details need recalling very carefully because they are sure to include sound advice from the highest intuitive part of your own self.

See also: CROSSROADS

KING   *A very important, distinguished character in your dream*

If this is not a real person known to you

The king in this case is probably one of the archetypes of the unconscious mind and represents a part of your own psyche that may have some important advice to impart. It is, perhaps, the seat of wisdom and accumulated knowledge. Think around all the details of the dream very carefully, and remember any particularly strong emotion which may have characterised your dream; the message it gives could be very useful in your life.

If a person known to you has taken on the trappings of a king

Only the dreamer can interpret his or her own dream thoroughly. If you dream that someone has become a king-like figure, this is probably how you are seeing them in waking life. A father figure, perhaps; or an unapproachable 'king of the castle'. It may be mere infatuation, but it could be that this person really does have something very important for your life and happiness.

See also: HERO; WISE PERSON

KITE

If you or someone else is flying a kite in your dream, it implies that something rather insubstantial is being kept aloft: an enterprise, perhaps, that is liable to collapse if there is a slight change of circumstances. The nature of the wind, like public opinion, is somewhat fickle, and the support your enterprise is receiving might suddenly disappear.

See also: GLIDER

LABYRINTH

Any dream situation where you find yourself in some kind of labyrinth or maze, implies that you are not 'lost'; you probably know where you are and where you want to go, but have arrived at a no-win situation with frustrations at every turn. In the family, at work, in society, it happens sometimes that whatever you try to do is likely to increase your problems, and your inner feelings see this situation as a virtual labyrinth. It may be a small problem, or it may encompass your whole life. If the dream itself offers no clues as to the best way forward, at least it is telling you to take an objective view of your difficulties.

See also: LOST

LADDER

The whole point of a ladder is to enable you to climb to a higher place, and in dreams this higher place is probably within your own mind. The self is often symbolised in dreams as a building. You normally live on the ground floor; your personal unconscious mind is downstairs in the basement; upstairs are your rarely visited higher intuitive faculties, or your intelligence when you really need to concentrate on some problem. If you very rarely visit the upper floor, and there may be no stairs in your dream house, this is where a ladder comes in useful. It is a means of escape from your own limitations. If you have been given the chance to explore the higher regions of your psyche, do not fail to take advantage of the situation.

See also: CLIMBING; ESCAPING

LAKE   or pond: enclosed water

Your dream lake may be dark and mysterious, or it may be sunlit and bright, depending perhaps on your own mood. Unless you have reason to dream about a real lake, this dream lake is probably an allegorical picture of your own self. Its depths represent your personal unconscious mind, and anything in, on or around it are likely to represent your own thoughts, feelings, ideas and impressions. The surface of the lake will represent your emotions, and these may be placid or disturbed. Perhaps you have had cause recently to think and feel very deeply about your life; if the water is muddy, perhaps you have been feeling guilty or uncertain as to the way ahead. These ideas need to be linked to any other features in the dream.

See also: DAM; SEA; WATER

LAMENESS

In dreams your feet represent your own journey through the world, as seen by the inner self. If you dream you have become lame, then plainly something is impeding your smooth progress. As always, there are at least two ways of looking at this: it could be your everyday, practical progress through life, and the lameness in your dream could be real, physical problems which trouble you; or it could be referring to your psychic progress. There may have been recent trigger events which gave rise to the symbol. These could involve a touch of envy, if others seem to be travelling through life and gaining success apparently effortlessly while you flounder. The same applies if someone else in your dream is showing lameness. They could be envying you in some respect. A feeling of patience in real life is required.

See also: FEET; JOURNEY

LAUNDRY

Dream clothes represent the personality and individual characteristics. Dirt connected with clothes implies faults and less-than-pleasant features associated with the people who wear them. A dream laundry represents a state of affairs that is intended to remove those stains, or actions that are intended to 'turn over a new leaf'. Soiled sheets carry a strong implication of guilt connected with bed and the bedroom. General dirt on household items, and furniture which is being cleaned implies that a person – either the dreamer or someone known to them personally – has been neglectful in some way, or their living conditions have been neglected to a disturbing degree.

See also: CLOTHES; DIRT

LIBRARY

Dream books normally represent knowledge or wisdom, unless they are plainly antique and valuable in their own right. A collection of books represents a source of knowledge which the dreamer relies upon. An individual book can symbolise a lifestyle, in the manner of a biography. Changing your library book in a dream suggests that you are about to change your lifestyle in some important way. Over and above these meanings, interpreting a dream about books depends very much on what books mean to the dreamer personally. To one person they may symbolise romance; to another adventure; to yet another academic study; and visiting a dream library may forecast an upturn in these activities.

See also: BOOKS

LILIES

Rather a specialised flower as a dream symbol: purity, virginity, death and funerals are frequently associated with them. In the example dream in chapter one a grandfather dreamed of buying lilies to symbolise that he was accepting the inevitability of death. Water lilies fill a different role: floating on the surface of water they can symbolise the innocent, unsuspecting, conscious self, blissfully unaware of the dark depths of the personal unconscious mind beneath them.

See also: FLOWER; FUNERAL; LAKE; WATER

LOST

It is a common experience to dream that you have become lost. The nature of having 'lost direction' depends on what 'direction' you consider paramount in your life. It may be an everyday case of having run up against problems in your professional or family life, or it may be much deeper than that: it may be referring to your spiritual progress through life, or having 'gone astray' in the religious sense. It sometimes happens that you dream of places familiar to you as a child, and think about going home, only to remember that you no longer live there. This dream symbol could be drawing your attention to the fact that there is more to life than the mere material aspects of physical existence; in this case you need to search for a spiritual dimension which will enable you to find the right direction in your waking life.

See also: LABYRINTH; UNEMPLOYED

LUGGAGE   *baggage, burdens which you need to carry*

In the dream world all life is a journey, and the baggage you carry with you comprises everything that has been acquired by your personality: loves and hates, hopes and fears, passions and desires, habits, customs, religious practices, prejudices and preconceptions. Perhaps it depends on how important the material things of the world are to you. Some people have acquired so much baggage that they can hardly move; others seem to be travelling light. If you dream that your own luggage is too heavy and burdensome, the time has come to lighten the load. You can do this by finding time to quieten your thoughts and emotions, and let go of all unnecessary trappings, all the things you become worked up about, all your strong dislikes and sorrows. Do you need them?

See also: OBSTACLES

MACHINERY   *Mechanical devices*

Anything of this nature in your dream is sure to represent some aspect of materiality, the workings of civilisation, industry, manufacturing, and impersonal progress. Disconcertingly large machines may be representing the possible opposition when you are beginning a new enterprise. You may be looking at these machines with a feeling of apprehension, perhaps wondering whether you can cope with their complicated controls. This is a fairly common situation when you are approaching some new situation in waking life, a new job, perhaps, when you are not sure whether you will fit in. It may simply be a matter of acquiring new technical skills. Another possibility is that you are looking with interest and want to become involved: perhaps you have been feeling left out of things. Or again the sight of machinery may repel you, and you want to escape from it and seek something more personal and peaceful: your own true self, perhaps!

See also: FACTORY

MANDALA

The 'magic circle' of a mandala derives from the Sanskrit, an ancient concept expressing the universal principle of the self. A circle, or a globe, very tellingly describes the process of dreaming, and the relationship between the conscious and unconscious minds. In dreams, a first realisation of the self as a spiritual principle will give rise to images reflecting this with regard to the dreamer's own normal everyday experiences. The self is not something new or alien, but the whole person, both inwardly and outwardly, and dreams depicting this will often feature a circle, or a square, or a combination of the two: a town square with flowers and trees; a group of dancers advancing and retreating to form a symmetrical pattern; an ancient stone circle; a flower with radiating petals. Images such as these may mark the commencement of a truly spiritual phase of your own life.

See also: CLOCK; FLOWER

MARKET   *or any busy, bustling place*

The dream market represents yourself meeting with the rest of society, interacting with people in the way normal to you. The symbol by itself expresses your attitude to others, and if it was merely an incident in a narrative dream, any strong emotions associated with it will be important. Some people need to mix and socialise more than they do; others need to cut down on social interaction. We may be gregarious creatures and we certainly need to be able to get along with other people, but on the other hand we all need to withdraw temporarily from society at times and spend a quiet meditative time alone.

See also: CARNIVAL; PLAYING

MIST   *the way ahead obscured*

Not quite as baffling as a heavy fog, but you still cannot see the way ahead clearly. The dream image is probably reflecting a state of affairs that has arisen in your waking life, when old certainties have turned into doubts. Patience is called for, and this is not a time for snap decisions. In due course a new direction and a better set of circumstances will present themselves as mist seldom lasts long. Wait until the way ahead is quite clear before making important decisions.

See also: CLOUDS; VALLEY

MONSTER

Something very frightening and quite unexpected has suddenly come to life. The chances are it has emerged from your own personal unconscious mind, a part of your own personal shadow, a set of characteristics you thought forgotten, a dark idea you thought safely in the past. A dream crocodile, or alligator, or an unknown horror may have emerged from the swamp and is seriously threatening your safety. It may be connected with someone else, a family member perhaps, who is behaving in a startling manner. If someone you know seems to have turned into a monster in your dream, it could be a very serious warning of psychological problems on the part of the person concerned. It sometimes happens that a bout of mental instability or insanity is heralded within the family by this dream image.

See also: ADVERSARY; DEMON; DRAGON;

MONUMENT   *a memorial built to impress*

A monument implies the wish that something or somebody should not be forgotten by posterity. This is the case with a war memorial,

210

for instance, or an impressive tombstone, or a statue set on a tall pillar. It is in effect trying to turn emotions into something solid. Emotions provide the key to the dream significance of this symbol. Something has affected the dreamer very deeply, something perhaps that he or she does not want to put into words, but which has taken on almost tangible solidity.

See also: IDOL; STATUE

MOON

One of the most ancient of dream symbols, along with sun, dawn, and night. Its meaning depends rather upon your own cultural background. In some cultures the moon is the great time-keeper; to others merely a comforting light in the dark. But to both it has a powerful emotional appeal, and may actually affect the human body in the way its gravity draws moisture towards itself: it certainly has a powerful effect on the tides of the ocean. To the dreamer it implies emotional reassurance.

See also: SUN

MOUNTAIN

If the mountain is a barrier or a threat

It may be a mountain range, or a cliff face, in effect forming a very high wall which is hemming you in and impeding your progress, possibly even threatening to fall on you and crush you. It is really a very clear symbol of some real-life circumstance which is having a similar effect: a material or even a psychological situation which is going to cause you problems.

If you are climbing the mountain

You may be 'scaling the heights of ambition', or hoping to do just that, or the dream mountain to be climbed may symbolise problems that you need to overcome, difficulties at work, or marital or family problems. You may be in danger of sliding back down the mountain, or you may have passed the peak and be on the way down. Ice and snow on the top implies that you are going through hard times which will soon improve. There should be no doubt in the dreamer's mind concerning the identity of this mountain in real life.

See also: CLIMBING

MUD

In dream symbolism, earth or soil represents solid materiality – the indisputable nature of facts as they really are. Water represents the emotions, and often the sexual desires. If there is mud along your path, the significance is that your way through life is being hampered by an excess of these feelings on your part. Sometimes a dream may picture you struggling through mud *alongside* a path or roadway. In some way you are following your own desires to an extent which is alarming even you, and you know you need to stop floundering and regain the hard road. Quite commonly a dream may have you driving or walking down an increasingly muddy track; you may even be in danger of becoming stuck permanently. The chances are that the meaning of dreams such as this will be perfectly obvious to you. Passions and desires can readily become a sticking point.

See also: DIRT; WATER

MUSEUM   *A display of old relics*

A museum display represents things and ideas that seem to you to be no longer of use, though they may once have been admired. In a real-life museum visitors are expected to be quiet and respectful,

212

almost reverent in the presence of values once held dear but now long gone. Is this the atmosphere of your dream? It may be that the dreamer is behaving badly in a museum, scoffing at the exhibits and upsetting the other visitors. In real life it is usually people and institutions with old-fashioned values that are symbolised by a dream museum, and the dreamer may be respectful in their presence, or scornful. What may seem to you a useless antique may still be of value to someone else: it could be that you are hurting someone's feelings in waking life.

See also: ANTIQUE; MORALITY

NAKED

Nakedness in a dream is portraying the person without the trappings of personality, the social veneer, the acquired habits and characteristics. Some people habitually see themselves as naked and unashamed during their dreams, because the inner feelings are showing them how they really are without any pretence. Inhibitions belong to the outer feelings; the inner feelings have no inhibitions. If you dream you are naked and feel the need to hide your nakedness, this means that in waking life you have been made to drop your social disguises against your will. People have seen through the social disguise of your persona and you are finding this an embarrassment.

See also: CLOTHES

OBSTACLES *barriers to progress*

Dream obstacles can take almost any form, but they all reflect real-life obstacles to the dreamer's smooth progress through life. They may be solidly material obstacles in the dream, but in waking life these obstacles are more likely to be purely psychological or social. The dream details need searching carefully for clues as to the real nature of these impediments. Quite often someone may dream that he or she is being pursued, but cannot make progress for whatever reason. The case is similar, and interpretation will depend on the symbolic reason for the handicap that is holding the dreamer back.

See also: CHASING; LUGGAGE

OPPONENT

Your dream opponent may of course be an actual person with whom you have problems, and the dream should be totally straight-forward. But if this is not the case, the type of opponent needs narrowing down and identifying: there are at least two alternative possibilities. The adversary is an opponent who has emerged from your own personal unconscious mind, an enigmatic figure composed perhaps of personal characteristics which trouble you but which you are not prepared to deal with in waking life. The assailant is a figure composed of factors from outside of yourself which have become symbolised as an individual opponent. The dream itself should offer clues to enable you to identify this threatening figure, and then perhaps you will be able to deal with the problem in waking life.

See also: ADVERSARY; ASSAILANT; NIGHTMARES

PAINTING

Applying covering coats of paint

Plainly something is being covered up and made to look different, possibly more attractive than it was before. Who is doing the painting in the dream, and what is being disguised? These are the crucial questions, and when these details have been established there should be no doubt about the meaning of the dream.

See also: ART; EMBROIDERY

PARROT

Parrots are acclaimed for their mimicry and are traditionally taught words and phrases, although obviously they will not understand what they are saying. This is the meaning of 'parrot' as a symbol. A schoolchild may 'parrot' words without having taken in their true significance, and a younger child just learning to speak may also copy sounds before learning their meaning: this is part of the natural learning process. To dream that a parrot sits on your or someone else's shoulder does not necessarily mean that you or they don't know what you're talking about. A dream of this nature sometimes happens when you are trying to learn to pronounce the unfamiliar sounds of a foreign language.

See also: BIRDS

PATH   *A way along which you walk*

This must be one of the most ancient of dream symbols, representing the dreamer's own way through life. In modern times, driving a car, riding a bike, or commuting by train in your dream will have much the same meaning, describing your normal daily progress and the difficulties and obstacles you may meet along the way. By itself, the dream symbol is no more than that – the fact or background of your own life. The factors to be met with along the path: the ease or difficulty with which you make progress, the nature of the surface, perhaps muddy, rough, rock-strewn, or covered with snow and ice; the people and things you encounter along the path, whether the path is well trodden or overgrown and remote, the scenery through which you walk – all these things will need analysing separately to form a picture of your own progress through life.

See also: CAR; DRIVING; FEET; JOURNEY; ROAD

215

PEARL

Actual pearls of course are produced by oysters, within their hard shell, and deep below the sea. Symbolically, a 'pearl of great price' is a non-material treasure hidden deep within the innermost emotions, beneath the sea of the unconscious mind. Even the mere awareness of such things is to be treasured: to complete the cyclic process of the personal unconscious mind and bring light to the darkest parts of the self may not be fully attainable, but to make progress in this direction is certainly a personal 'pearl' of inestimable value.

See also: GOLD; JEWELS; TREASURE

PIG

As a symbol the pig has a variable significance depending upon the race, the religion or the cultural background of the person concerned. Because it was foremost on the list of proscribed animals as presented by Moses, within those religions that follow Moses to this day it can be perceived as something to be shunned. People of other cultures were taught that the words which come out of one's mouth can be far more damaging to one's spiritual status than the food which goes in, and for them the pig lost its unclean status. To many people the pig has always represented a major part of their staple diet, and is thought of in familiar terms. As a domesticated animal both greedy and intelligent, as a wild boar fierce and untamed, or as a pink and naked piglet symbolic perhaps of sexual peccadilloes, there are many types of people who can be symbolised by a pig in dream imagery.

See also: ANIMALS

PIT   *Any unidentified hole in the ground*

Like the abyss, this is one of the most basic of dream symbols, representing the personal unconscious mind. Matters which have not been fully dealt with by the conscious mind pass down into the dark recesses of the unconscious. As a dream symbol it may warn against the un-wisdom of throwing unwanted objects into the pit, hoping to see the last of them, because they will not simply disappear. If they are not matters which can be dealt with by the inner feelings and re-presented to the conscious mind in the form of dreams, they are liable to form part of the shadow that lurks in the lowest, darkest part of the psyche. A dream pit may be warning of the need to deal with matters as they arise, and not hope that they will go away by simply ignoring them.

See also: ABYSS; CELLAR; GORGE

PLAYING

If you are watching without taking part

Whatever the nature of the game, others are presumably enjoying the activity and you, the dreamer, are on the fringe. The question is, do you want to join in or not, and if not, why are you standing watching? The game may be symbolising the rat-race of life from which you have thankfully retired; or you may have been feeling shut out from the social and business scene and would like nothing better than to be admitted. what are your feelings on the matter?

If you are taking part in the game

Again, the game is likely to symbolise the hurly-burly of life, and it is your own attitude towards the game and the other players that will hold the significance of the dream. The theme mood or overriding emotion which you may have felt on waking and recalling the dream will give you the clue. Did you enjoy taking part, or would you have preferred to walk away and leave it?

See also: BALL; CARNIVAL; MARKET; PROCESSION

PLOUGHING *Carving a furrow in the ground*

Earth represents materiality, the potential from which you can create the wherewithal of life, build a business empire, rear a family. If you are a farmer, ploughing can represent next year's income and your future welfare. It is an age-old symbol, of course, and a well-ploughed field is a sign of satisfaction and security. If things go wrong during the process, you keep turning up stones perhaps, or find you are disturbing vicious ants or other creatures, the symbols involved will have significance for the future and should be interpreted accordingly.

See also: DESERT; DIGGING; EARTH MOTHER

POLICE

Out-and-out criminals or persecuted minorities may have a different perception; but for the majority of people a policeman represents a principle for the good. Most people care about their own characters, and would prefer others to see them as basically good rather than bad, and a dream policeman in their case will represent a guardian of good conduct. If you have feelings of guilt about anything at all, a dream policeman may be watching you suspiciously. To follow unspoken rules of conduct through life is not the same as excessive morality or 'do-gooding': it is to achieve and maintain a fair balance in your own psyche. Your inner feelings, as your own seat of conscience, are interested in all your actions and thoughts for this purpose. All people are psychically linked on that deep level, and to hurt another in any way is the same as hurting yourself: this is why no-one can escape the consequences of his or her actions in the long run. The symbolic policeman is watching you! To dream you are carrying a friendly policeman in your car implies that you have made or are about to make a morally correct decision.

See also: MORALITY; UNIFORM

PRECIPICE   *A steep drop down*

There are numerous symbols of the unconscious mind, the edge of awareness over which all your unwanted and half-forgotten ideas fall out of sight – but not out of mind. But this stark symbol may be more practical: if the track you are following ends on the edge of a cliff, the warning could scarcely be clearer: there will be problems ahead if you continue on your present course. In either case the symbol is a warning to the dreamer, whether in physical or in psychological terms: take careful stock of where you are heading and look before you leap. You cannot continue as you are.

> *See also:*   ABYSS; GORGE; PIT

PROCESSION

If you are taking part in the dream procession

Were you happy to be following the crowd during the dream? The symbol is rather suspect: you are being swept along by what seems to be the majority view; individuals in a procession do not decide where they are going, or how fast, and they are not in a position to change their minds. It might be better for you to hold back and rethink your own position. Majority decisions tend to echo the lowest and narrowest rather than the highest or broadest of viewpoints.

If you are watching the procession without taking part

The symbol of a procession seems to be expressing the popular view, and the fact that you are watching with interest without joining in implies that you want to remain independent. You may or may not agree with the popular cause; the nature of the procession, the people taking part and the other symbols involved, should explain the meaning of the dream.

> *See also:*   CARNIVAL

QUARREL

Usually in a quarrel, both sides believe they are in the right and the other person is in the wrong. But it may be that neither side is in the right; or it may be that both sides are right, and simply using different sets of words and ideas to express the same truth: they will probably be using different *symbols* with a common interpretation. Dreaming about a real situation involving a quarrel usually means that the dreamer has made a misjudgement of some kind; to dream of a symbolic or allegorical quarrel in which you are taking part usually means that you, the dreamer, have been misled by your own pride. The inner feelings see things as they are, without pride, and may be advising you to make amends if you have wronged somebody unintentionally.

See also: ABUSE; ACCUSATIONS; ANGER

QUEEN

If you are the queen in your dream

The regal figure you have become may represent yourself as you would like others to see you, and how you like to think of yourself. It could be a portrayal of your own persona, your social mask which is becoming a little too powerful, a little too convincing for your own good.

If the dream queen is a person known to you

Plainly this person has made a very strong impression on your waking mind. Do you want her to behave like a queen? And what is your attitude towards her: admiration, worship, or servitude? The meaning of a dream such as this should be obvious to the dreamer. If it is not, it may be that the person who has become a queen in your dream, has something of real value to offer you, and you should not turn it down.

If the dream queen is quite unknown to you

This dream figure could be one of the archetypes of the unconscious mind. If you are a woman, she will have some very valuable advice to offer, and you need to study the dream carefully in order to discover exactly what it is. It will be related to your own recent waking experiences. If you are a man, this enigmatic dream figure could be the *anima*, the intuitive part of your own psyche that can help you to understand the female mind and your relationships with the opposite sex in particular. Again, your own recent experiences will help you interpret the dream.

See also: GODDESS; WISE PERSON

RAIL JOURNEY

If you normally commute by train

This will probably equate to your normal journey through life in the same way as driving, the road, or a path usually does. It will probably be an everyday dream recalling or foretelling of encounters with friends, foes or colleagues.

If you very rarely travel by train

Where driving a car nowadays usually represents a mere extension of the legs, expressing your normal day-to-day journey through life, a rail journey is likely to signify a major transition. It implies being separated by a long distance, and travelling abroad or returning to your own country is often symbolised in dreams by a rail trip. Similarly it can symbolise a change of lifestyle rather than mere location. The imminent appearance in your life of someone from long ago or far away, or an associate with an unfamiliar approach to life, is often heralded by dreaming of their arrival by train. You may be meeting them at the station.

See also: JOURNEY

RAINBOW

This most beautiful of natural phenomena associated with the weather tends to appear against dark clouds when rainstorms are abating, and so inevitably it symbolises the end of a difficult period and the beginning of better times. It can also have a different meaning: as rainbow colours are the separate components of pure white light, they can represent divided parts of any whole. The human race with all its diverse people and cultures can be depicted in dreams in this way. It can symbolise people in general, different types, different races, or perhaps merely various types of personality, represented by different colours. Someone in a dream who is shown as being frightened of the rainbow is being portrayed as one who shuns society for psychological reasons.

See also: CLOUDS

RATS

A few people like rats and keep them as pets, but the great majority see them as pests, suspect them of carrying diseases, and find them disgusting. The truth is, they are just animals trying to live their lives in peace, but their way of life inevitably brings them into close contact with humans. If a rat could speak, it would probably say that it would prefer to be domesticated, like a dog. As a dream symbol, the rat normally arouses strong feelings, as it does in real life. In fact a dream rat symbolises these feelings. Whatever the dreamer normally feels about rats, any real-life incident that invokes similar feelings may be expressed in a dream as an invasion of rats. The dream rat can become a symbol of your own behaviour if you have acted in what you yourself might consider to be a rat-like manner.

See also: ANIMALS

RIVER *Running water*

The flow of emotions, or of sexual desires, or even of life itself. In the religious sense it can represent the Holy Spirit, and several real-life rivers in the world have religious significance to many people. In their dreams the river will represent their own fulfilment or hopes for the future. To Christians, the Jordan River for centuries has represented the barrier between life and death. The image of living on the banks of a river may represent someone who is suppressing his or her sexual desires. To someone making a study of their dream life, the river in a dream may be seen as something to be crossed, sooner or later. On a more mundane level, a dream river that is in flood symbolises turbulent sexual feelings of which the dreamer is rather afraid. A gentle flow of clear water implies that one's conscience is clear.

See also: FORD; BRIDGE; WATER

ROAD   The *way along which you and others travel*

The course of your life is often depicted in dreams as a road along which you travel. The surface of the road may be smooth, or pot-holed, or muddy, or rock-strewn, symbolising the obstacles you meet from day to day. The dream road may be narrow or broad, straight or winding. Everything and everyone you encounter on your dream journey reflects the incidents that happen to you in real life, and need to be interpreted accordingly.

See also: DRIVING; PATH; RAIL JOURNEY

ROCKS

A rocky, stony place that you have to travel through usually represents temporary hardships in real life that you have to endure. Rocks are always a symbol of solid materiality, lacking in spiritual

223

content, and this can be taken in numerous ways. The symbol can refer to other uncaring people who are making life difficult, or to matters of health that cause you problems. It can imply that you are lacking in spiritual motivation and need to look beyond mere material profit and loss. Something similar is implied by a solitary towering rock in your dream: it is a symbol of the self – your own psychic centre, which has become rock-bound and inflexible through excessive materiality. The dream might be advising you to be less hard and unyielding in your outlook.

See also: MOUNTAIN; ROAD; STONE CIRCLE

RUINS   *A building no longer in use*

Rather a poignant symbol, reflecting past glories and certainties long gone. But a building can also symbolise oneself, or some other person, and a ruined building can represent someone on whom you used to rely, but is no longer available: a parent, perhaps. It can also represent an organization of some kind, which is no longer to be depended upon, or attitudes which belong to the past and cannot be recaptured.

See also: ABBEY

SAND

The earth, the soil, represents the material background to our lives, and sand is totally barren. When life-giving water falls on sand usually it either drains away very quickly or forms a quagmire, and any life form will find it very difficult to survive there. To dream you are struggling through sandy desert implies a complete lack of power, or any sense of power. When you consider the world dream and refer also to Adlerian dreams you will see that plants struggling to take roothold in the desert are like humans striving after a modicum of power for themselves – people who are feeling helpless in the face of overwhelming odds. Nobody likes a pushy person, but perhaps the dream symbol is telling you to be more assertive in your dealings with others; it is no use depending on their goodwill.

See also: DESERT; SWAMP

SCRAPHEAP

A collection of junk and old items that people no longer have use for. They may perhaps be recyclable and turned into something useful, but they are not items you want cluttering up your house. The self is sometimes symbolised in dreams as a house, and it may be that this junk consists of old ideas, bad habits, past values, worn-out relationships that are no longer relevant to your life. It is time they were cleared out, and your lifestyle given an airing.

See also: LUGGAGE; OBSTACLES; PIT

SEA

If you are connected with the sea in your everyday life, to dream of the sea may be simply placing the dream on an everyday basis. But if there is no obvious connection, remember that water symbolises human emotions, including the sexual urges. The other features and people in the dream should give you the clue. You may be swimming or merely paddling in these powerful feelings. You may be out of your depth and drowning in them. You may be able to float over them with impunity; you may even be able to swallow the whole sea, to imply that you have risen above and can well cope with all these emotional passions. The sea can also symbolise the unfathomable collective unconscious mind, and if your dream is a dawn dream, a great dream perhaps, this may be the significance of it. Swim in this sea with caution: remember that everything it contains are collective phenomena and not your own personal contents. To believe otherwise is to court psychological inflation and long-term disillusionment.

See also: DROWNING; WATER

SKELETON

This framework of bones is a term used to mean the basic material framework of almost anything, not merely the remains of a human being, but the basic layout of any scheme, material or abstract, before the details have been added. So in a non-human or non-animal context, it symbolises the raw beginnings of some project that may be developed into something substantial. In the human and animal sense, however, it symbolises the last remaining traces of what was once a living, functioning being. Usually, as a dream symbol, it refers to the latter: the mortal remains of what was once a living, breathing, possibly spiritual person. A *memento mori*, if you find a skeleton in your dream it probably refers to human relationships and influence long gone.

See also: ARCHEOLOGY; BONES; CORPSE

SNAKE

An ancient symbol in many cultures, and with several different meanings. In the biblical Book of Genesis the snake is the first tempter of mankind, offering judgment and intelligence instead of a purely instinctive way of life. A snake might symbolise eternal youth, or even eternal life, as indicated by the sloughing of its skin. It is a symbol of untrustworthiness because of the way in which it may slither unseen through the grass, a hidden danger. It can symbolise lust, through its sinuous, phallic shape. A dream snake seems to be offering a warning not to trust somebody or something – or could it be you, the dreamer, who is acting in this way?

See also: ANIMALS

SNOW AND ICE

Fortunately, snow and ice melt after a while when warmer weather arrives. As a dream symbol the implication is that the emotional atmosphere surrounding the dreamer is cold and frosty, but the expectations are that this cold atmosphere will thaw out before too long and relationships start to improve. Walking through cold, snowy conditions implies that the dreamer can expect times to be difficult and somewhat uncomfortable for a while, though an improvement will take place before long. A dream with snow seems to be advising the dreamer to be patient. A child's dream of snow. on the other hand, may speak only of pleasure and not hardship.

See also: FROST; GLACIER

STATUE

The likeness of a person carved in stone or some other material – this could be a representation of the self, or of some aspect of the self that has become petrified and frozen with disuse, possibly one of the archetypes of the unconscious mind. Someone who has been behaving in what the rest of the world perceives as an outrageous manner will seem to be out of touch with the sensitivities of others: perhaps his or her persona has taken on this symbolically uncaring or uncooperative form. A solitary standing stone may carry much the same significance. Whether the dream symbol refers to the dreamer personally or to some other figure, the person concerned seems to be lacking in emotional rapport. When the dream statue is of some famous figure from the past, it could be that the dreamer has been taking an interest in or attaching undue importance to matters which are no longer valid. There could be a phallic significance, particularly when the statue becomes small enough to be held in the hand.

See also: CARVINGS; IDOL

STEPPING STONES   *The means to cross water dry-footed*

In dreams a stream to be crossed usually represents the flow of emotions and sexual attraction, which in this case the dreamer feels needs to be resisted. Wading across means that the dreamer is sampling these powerful feelings without becoming overly influenced by them. Crossing by means of a bridge implies that he or she wishes to avoid contact with these emotions altogether. Stepping stones represent the middle way: one is close enough to the water to study it carefully and take an interest in it, yet still remain unaffected by the flow of feelings which it symbolises.

See also: FORD; RIVER; WATER

STONE CIRCLE   *A circular ancient monument*

These prehistoric monuments are widespread in parts of Europe and particularly perhaps in the British Isles. It is in Ireland, Wales, England and Scotland that this dream symbol is sometimes experienced. Stonehenge is a famous but not at all typical example: most of them are simply rough circles of rocks to be found in hilly country and wild areas. Whatever the motives of the people who constructed them, in dreams they can be seen as a mandala of the self, particularly in its relation to the world and the solar system. It can also signify the family circle, especially when this tends to be hidebound and unyielding. People who have been seeking a spiritual 'way' may dream of having to pass through the circle in some way, arriving at a new level of understanding.

See also: ARCHEOLOGY; DOOR; ROCKS

STORE

A building or container filled with all sorts of goods may represent the personal unconscious mind, the place normally hidden and closed where all your experiences and impressions are stored. To visit and rummage through this store in your dream is good: it implies that the cycle of the dreaming self is working well. But a store or shop may also symbolise materiality – the 'lowest' end of the spiritual hierarchy, but the place where all sorts of good things are available. If you are on the way 'down' you may arrive at this store with a feeling of expectation. If you are on the way 'up' and following a spiritual path, you will be leaving this store behind.

See also: BARN

SUN

As the prime giver of life to the earth, the sun must be one of the most ancient of dream symbols. The rising sun equates to a new dawn, new hopes, new possibilities, the rebirth of the psyche to a new understanding, a new level of being. Dark deeds are uncovered by the sun, so it is a symbol of openness and honesty. Wealth and material success are symbolised by sunshine. Darkness speaks of death and disaster, loss of health and wealth. But a setting sun rarely predicts disaster: it marks the passing of the established order and promises peace and respite. Where danger lurks the arrival of darkness can also symbolise safety. It is so very basic a symbol that when it features in a dream it is probably merely highlighting whatever the dream itself portrays.

See also: ECLIPSE

SUNDIAL

The dial itself is a mandala symbol, probably representing the self under the influence of time: the march of progress and the inevitability of fate. The upright pedestal is an ancient phallic symbol, probably less in evidence nowadays than when people were less open about their sexual desires, but still a potent symbol of regeneration and the continuity of life. The sundial suggests a certain closeness to nature and a clinging to old ways. The time it shows is the only true time known to nature, the time based on the movements of our planet in relation to the sun, rather than the sophisticated averaged-out time of modern civilisation. As a dream symbol, like a clock, the sundial can express urgency and the transitory nature of life. It can also represent an ancient set of values that is still valid, and which would be of great benefit.

See also: CALENDAR; CLOCK

TEETH

When you have toothache you might dream of something unpleasant happening to your teeth – a quite understandable reaction when pain is nagging at your conscious awareness, even in your sleep. But many people dream that their teeth are broken or missing when they are perfectly sound. Somebody said to be 'toothless' is unable to react as he or she would like, and this is the probable implication of toothlessness as a dream symbol. Perhaps somebody has been provoking the dreamer in real life, taking advantage of the apparent lack of retaliation.

See also: BULLY

THEATRE

A theatrical performance is not the place to look for sincerity, and the point about actors is that they are pretending to be something or somebody which they are not. It is also a place of entertainment, however, so theatrical deception is unlikely to be malicious. A dream theatre is not representing truth, and though the characters in it are not to be taken at their face value, they may be offering a new perspective on an old problem, suggesting a light-hearted attitude towards the possibility of tolerating problematic circumstances which cannot be dealt with in any other way.

See also: ACTING

THRONE   *The seat of majesty*

If you are seated on the throne

There seems to be something not quite right about the idea of seeing yourself enthroned in splendour. You are plainly being symbolised as superior over others, but in what way? Search the dream very carefully for clues, because clearly you cannot sit on the throne with sincerity.

If someone you know is seated on the throne

This person may genuinely have something of great value to offer if you are prepared to accept their superiority in some regard. On the other hand, this may simply be *your* opinion of what you suppose *their* opinion of themselves to be.

If a stranger is sitting on the throne

The dream needs exploring carefully for further clues. It may be that the person sitting on the throne is one of the archetypes of the unconscious mind, in which case the message they convey may be of the greatest value to your waking mind.

See also: ARCHETYPES; KING; QUEEN

TIDAL WAVE   *A wall of water or a tsunami*

A great wave of emotion, and more particularly an immense surge of sexual desires, these are things over which we have little control, and if they are worrying us we are liable to dream of them in this way. If you are confronted with a great wall of water about to engulf you in a dream, note particularly what effect it had, not only on you but on any other people and objects round about. If you are swept away and find yourself in difficulties, it seems that an urgent reappraisal of your lifestyle is overdue. If however it leaves you unaffected and dry, though other characters nearby may be swept away, the dream message is that although the way ahead may prove daunting and difficult at times, you will eventually overcome your problems.

See also: DROWNING; WATER

TOILET

It is quite a common dream experience: you need to go to the toilet fairly urgently, but cannot find one that is usable: it doesn't work, it's not properly plumbed in, it's too dirty, or too much in the public gaze. In other words, your body wants to get rid of your waste material, but can't. There may be a very simple and practical explanation: you want to go without bothering to wake up, and your inner feelings are pointing out that you can't do that. But if you don't really need to go that badly, there may be quite another reason for the dream: the waste matter you need to get rid of may be psychological clutter, or perhaps bad habits and faults which are holding you back and blocking the free cycle of the dreaming self. You know you ought to get rid of them, but it is far easier to find excuses for hanging on. There are no moral implications in this; the dream is simply drawing your attention to the state of affairs existing within your own psyche.

See also: EXCREMENT

TOWER   *A tall strong building*

Of course, there are several types of tower. There is the tower block of flats which can merely set the scene for an everyday relationship dream. Or when someone is setting out in business and is somewhat nervous of the potential competition, he or she may dream of towering office blocks and industrial buildings which make the dreamer feel small. Commonly, however, a stout tower represents the family, or marriage. A 'tower of strength' on which we ought to be able to rely, and one in which we can hide if needs be. You may dream you are outside such a building and wandering how you can get in, because you have been searching for security in real life. Or if you dream you are inside the tower you may perhaps be dreading what is in the cellar or the dungeons below ground, or wishing that you could gain access to the uppermost rooms. This is because most people live in one dimension – above their own personal unconscious mind and below their own higher psychological and spiritual possibilities.

See also: BATTLEMENTS; FORTRESS

TREASURE

If you have actually found treasure in your dream

You may have had a stroke of good fortune recently, whether of a material nature or purely a matter of wellbeing and peace of mind; in either case you will be sure to know what the symbol means without trying to analyse it further. If it is not obvious, however, you will need to think through the dream details very carefully to find out its true nature.

If you are searching for the treasure which you know to be near

The dream is probably referring to a spiritual or psychological treasure which is already present within your own psyche. If another person known to you features in the dream, he or she will have been or is about to be instrumental in helping you find the treasure. When you start to record and pay attention to your dreams, you will know that a great treasure is the ultimate discovery: there can be few treasures on earth more important than the discovery of your own soul.

See also: DRAGON; GOLD; JEWELS; PEARL

TUNNEL   *Travelling underground*

The road or path symbolises your own journey through life, and when this plunges below ground or runs through a patch of darkness, you have temporarily lost sight of your surroundings or the way ahead. If in your dream you were aware of a glimmer of light ahead, your position will soon be made plain and new understanding is sure to ensue. If not, and when all analysis yields no further clues, patience and a sense of submission is called for. It may be portraying a real situation at work or in society where you are running through a difficult patch. Or it may represent your own personal unconscious mind where your normal thought processes can see nothing. If this dream is persistent and worrying, it may be pointing ahead to medical problems, or a temporary loss of full normal consciousness. Tunnels don't go on forever, and any trauma of this nature will probably prove to be a temporary glitch.

See also: ABYSS; DARKNESS

UNEMPLOYMENT

Real unemployment, or a feeling of having nothing to do, no useful function to perform, can have a depressing effect. An economic depression in the country can result in increased clinical depression among the people, and a play on words like this is frequently to be found in dreams. When somebody is feeling depressed, they may well dream of unemployment, though they may have no shortage of work in fact. A major cause of depression is an awareness of one's inability to be true to oneself: for whatever reason, your true nature may not fit in with the lifestyle you are obliged to lead. Everyone is unique, and the only way by which one can reach higher awareness – especially spiritual attainment – is being true to one's own inner self. To 'atone' means being 'at one' in every sense. A dream of unemployment may be telling you to be true or honest to your own inner character: 'Know then thyself!'

See also: LOST

UNIFORM *Conforming in dress*

Dressing uniformly is a token of involvement, or belonging to a certain class or group. Even a 'fashion uniform' means that you are associating yourself with others of a similar turn of mind. At school, in the services, and various types of employment, a uniform represents equality and conformity. As a dream symbol it can represent some organisation or power which has an influence on your waking life. If you wear a uniform in real life, this could be called your normal dress. But if you dream of wearing a uniform when this is not the case, it implies that you have been acting in the way that others expect you to act, or are being forced into the same fate as others. This is particularly significant if you consider yourself an individualist and like to be different. Perhaps the dream is pointing out that your individuality is being compromised in some way.

See also: CLOTHES; FASHIONS

VALLEY

Solid earth represents materiality, and to dream you are in a valley implies that you are penned in by a material situation. When the valley is shrouded in mist or fog, you will be unable to see your way clearly, either to go on or to go back. The dream symbol may be referring to a matter of physical health, when you are helpless to do anything about it; or it might refer to a dead-end situation at work, or confines of some kind from which it seems there is no easy escape. If you cannot think of any parallel in real life, take it as a friendly warning not to become involved in anything involving too firm a commitment, a situation from which you will not be able to retreat. If you have had anything to do with the occult, or spiritualism, or some extreme political view, it would be better for you to turn your back on these things, and seek a more open and perhaps truly spiritual influence in your life.

See also: JOURNEY; ROAD; ROCKS

VASE   *or similar ornamental container*

The concept of a personal vase which you would like people to admire, or in which you can place flowers to beautify your surroundings, is closely related to the concept of the persona, which represents that part or aspect of yourself that you would like others to see; the way in which you would like them to think of you. But the vase is more personal and individual than that: it is only meant to be seen and admired by those close to you whom you particularly wish to impress. As a dream symbol it crops up chiefly in romantic situations, representing your regard for the other party.

See also: BARN; CUP; STORE

VOLCANO

The symbolic mountain that 'blows its top' describes a material and apparently peaceful situation that is liable to turn dangerous if taken too much for granted. It may feature within marriage, or at work, or any situation where other people's feelings and patience may be stretched to the limit. There may be trouble ahead, or a major change in personal lifestyle.

See also: EARTHQUAKE

WALL   *A solid barrier*

A dream wall may be a barrier to your progress, but it may be simply a guide to steer you along the best path. There may be a way through or over the wall if you follow it. Your current course through life may possibly be in question, and a barrier may turn out to be a help rather than a hindrance. Although it may refer to something in the nature of a psychological barrier impeding your forward progress, or interference by uncooperative people in real life, a wall can be a safety measure too, keeping out unwanted influences, or blocking off a dangerous path.

See also: FENCE; HEDGE

WATER

The flow of emotions

There are many forms that the water symbol can take – the sea, waves, rivers, streams, lakes, ponds, or wells, or drinking water in a cup or the hollow of the hand. Personal interpretation of the whole dream should never be neglected, even if the meaning of the symbol itself seems obvious. The feelings or the emotions are symbolised in dreams by water, and it follows that the clarity or murkiness of the dream water is significant. Psychological clutter that has not yet been dealt with in the personal unconscious mind and feelings of guilt that have not been in some way atoned will darken and discolour the water with mud. Clear water, perhaps with coral, shells and clean pebbles signifies crystal-clear emotions, a clear conscience, with not too many psychological blocks. Murky water featuring in your dream-life suggests that you should begin to take your own inner condition seriously, beginning by recording and analysing your dreams assiduously. The first step towards solving a problem is acknowledging that a problem exists.

Sexual desire symbolised by water

In the traditional symbolism of the East a hermit living on the banks of a mighty river represents one who practices celibacy. The river represents his sexual desires, and he is able to watch it rolling past without wishing to plunge in. In Western symbolism a river can represent death, and finally crossing this river implies leaving behind one's life and all the desires associated with it: birth, sex, and death are all closely related in the world of symbolism. To dream of experiencing difficulties in crossing a river or stream, implies that you are reluctant to abandon emotional attachments, and in particular old sexual habits that you might be better off without. It can also mean that the dreamer is unwilling to face his or her own emotions when these seem too deep, and tends to switch off and become detached when emotional subjects are raised.

The lake of the inner self

A lake, a pond, any restricted area of water is likely to symbolise the inner self, or more specifically the unseen and unfathomable depths of the personal unconscious mind. A flower such as a water lily floating on the surface as a dream image could be pointing out that the dreamer has been placing too much reliance on his or her intellect; possibly by practising self control and following moral restrictions which might be better relaxed. No-one should neglect the deep water of the unconscious mind while seeing only the water lily above. In the depth of this dream lake lurks the shadow, gaining in strength and feeding on the detritus that floats to the bottom. The personal unconscious mind may also be symbolised by a well, which carries the idea of a store of wisdom waiting to be drawn from this well and drunk. To dream of drinking water implies that you are taking in whatever is being symbolised by the water.

The collective unconscious symbolised by water

A vast ocean rather than a pond, this is a symbol of the collective unconscious which, although available to the inner feelings is shared equally by the whole of humankind. This is a sea of wisdom, and the source of the archetypes of the unconscious mind which can impart the best advice; but although it is good to become familiar with its contents it can be dangerous to swim in this sea. People have become possessed, as it were, by images from the collective unconscious, falsely believing them to be personal attributes. In plain language, this means that they become inflated with their own importance and believe themselves to be some kind of super-person. A gentle sip of water from this great sea, on the other hand, is only ever beneficial: a taste of wisdom whilst appreciating good advice,

See also: BOAT; BRIDGE; DAM; FORD; LAKE;
RIVER; STEPPING STONES; TIDAL WAVE

WEEDING

Particularly if you ever practice gardening in real life, you may recognise weeding as a dream image, possibly with no other symbols involved in the dream. When we become aware of the need to shed the various faults and weaknesses that have invaded the territory of the inner feelings, and on discovering that it is impossible to do this using the mind and emotions in the usual way, we are liable to dream of weeding a flower bed. Invasive plants with long underground roots, weeds becoming matted inextricably in the roots of prize plants, weeds which sprawl over the top of other plants and smother them, these are succinct images. A great deal of tweaking and separation of invasive roots is needed, and this symbolises the work done by the inner feelings.

See also: DIRT; EXCREMENT

WISE PERSON   *An unknown person who gives advice*

If a real person known to the dreamer gives them the benefit of his or her advice in a dream, the value of that advice is certainly in question. But an unknown wise person is likely to be one of the archetypes of the unconscious mind, representing the highest, intuitive part of the dreamer's own psyche. In this case the advice will be sound, though the dream will need careful interpretation according to the dreamer's own experiences and needs. This dream figure may appear as a well-dressed bystander of authority, a doctor, or a teacher, or possibly the dreamer's own father.

See also: HERO; KING; QUEEN

WITCH   *A woman with unpleasant characteristics*

Some women may think of 'witch' in terms of 'wicca', in the sense of 'personal goddess' or even 'female empowerment', but this is not what I mean by the dream witch. The dream witch is the female counterpart of a demon or a devil, and is a manifestation of the shadow. This frightening character will consist of matters that have been pushed into the personal unconscious mind, thoughts, feelings and impressions that seemed unacceptable to the conscious awareness: all the disturbing ideas and negative emotions that should have been dealt with as they arose, but were denied recognition. These matters will have been gathering strength until they emerge in dreams in this guise; they may also be identified as a 'night hag', or nightmare.

See also: DEMON; GODDESS; NIGHTMARE

WOLF

Over the centuries wolves have been demonised and given a bad name, as all wild dogs tend to be, although they are probably not an actual risk to humans. A 'wolf' can mean a womanising man; a 'wolf in sheep's clothing' is a hidden danger; to 'keep the wolf from the door' is to avoid starvation; to 'throw somebody to the wolves' is to make a scapegoat of them, and a 'wolf pack' can refer to any marauding gang. All these meanings may be associated with the wolf as a dream symbol: it implies something we are afraid of and cannot control.

See also: ANIMALS

XENOPHOBIA

The fear or unreasonable hatred of foreigners as a dream theme has unfortunately become more common since the terrorist atrocities and threats of recent times. As a dream symbol it involves becoming alarmed by some unknown and seemingly suspicious figure or figures approaching or surrounding the dreamer. Sometimes it is little more than apprehension: a feeling of being threatened by someone who does actually appear in the dream. This falls into the category of dream opponent, or more specifically a dream assailant – an actual threat from a real person or thing. There is also an element of the dream adversary, because the root of this fear may lie within the dreamer's own psyche, without involving an actual threat. If there is a lesson to be learnt from a xenophobic dream, it must be to avoid unreasonable attitudes and behaviour, or un-thought-out reactions aimed at perceived outsiders.

See also: ADVERSARY; ASSAILANT; BURGLAR; ENEMY; GHOST; OPPONENT

YOKE   *A work-device for the shoulders*

This is an ancient symbol of servitude, slavery, drudgery, forced labour, and the general feeling of being exploited and hard done by. It often appears in family or marital dreams, particularly when the female of a relationship feels used and unappreciated. In dreams the yoke may appear simply as a carved piece of wood unrecognised for what it is, or something to be carried on the shoulder. It may also appear in the form of a wedding present of uncertain usage.

See also: LOST; OBSTACLES; TOWER

ZOO   *A place where non-domestic animals are kept*

In a sense, people are animals, being largely governed by animal-type instincts and automatic reactions, and a dream zoo or perhaps a safari park may represent the animal instincts of people in general. Family squabbles often follow these lines, equating the quarrelling relatives with animals. The symbol of a zoo may well appear in a dream when the dreamer has moved to a new area, a new job, a new school, a new type of society, where the other people involved seem to be less moral and more sexually expressive than had been expected. They are behaving 'like a lot of animals'. This depends on the dreamer's perceptions of others. But as a dream symbol the zoo could be reflecting the world dream. The 'animal' section is quite well advanced, so as a dream symbol the zoo could represent a desirable place to be, and an ideal stepping-off point from which ambitions could well be achieved.

See also: ANIMALS; FARM

INDEX

www.ingramcontent.com/pod-product-compliance
Lightning Source LLC
Chambersburg PA
CBHW060504090426
42735CB00011B/2107